LifeLight

"In Him was life, and that life was the light of men." John 1:4

Genesis, Part 2

—

GENESIS 25:12–50:26

LEADERS GUIDE

CPH
SAINT LOUIS

Earl H. Gaulke, editor

Revised from material prepared by Dean O. Wenthe and Timothy Huber

This publication is available in braille and in large print for the visually impaired. Write to the Library for the Blind, 1333 S. Kirkwood Road, St. Louis, MO 63122-7295; or call 1-800-433-3954.

Copyright © 2001 by Concordia Publishing House
3558 S. Jefferson Ave., St. Louis, MO 63118-3968
Manufactured in the U.S.A.

Cover Illustration: Eric Westbrook

Contents

Introduction

Welcome to LifeLight

A special pleasure is in store for you. You will be instrumental in leading your brothers and sisters in Christ closer to Him who is our life and light (John 1:4). You will have the pleasure of seeing fellow Christians discover new insights and rediscover old ones as they open the Scriptures and dig deep into them, perhaps deeper than they have ever dug before. More than that, you will have the pleasure of sharing in this wonderful study.

LifeLight—An In-depth Study

LifeLight is a series of in-depth Bible studies. The goal of LifeLight is that through a regular program of in-depth personal and group study of Scripture, more and more Christian adults may grow in their personal faith in Jesus Christ, enjoy fellowship with the members of His body, and reach out in love to others in witness and service.

In-depth means that this Bible study includes the following four components: individual daily home study; discussion in a small group; a lecture presentation on the Scripture portion under study; and an enhancement of the week's material (through reading the enrichment magazine).

LifeLight Participants

LifeLight participants are adults who desire a deeper study of the Scriptures than is available in the typical Sunday morning adult Bible class. (Mid-to-older teens might also be LifeLight participants.) While LifeLight does not assume an existing knowledge of the Bible or special experience or skills in Bible study, it does assume a level of commitment that will bring participants to each of the nine weekly assemblies having read the assigned readings and attempted to answer the study questions. Daily reading and study will require from 15 to 30 minutes for the five days preceding the

LifeLight assembly. The day following the assembly will be spent reviewing the previous week's study by going over the completed study leaflet and the enrichment magazine.

LifeLight Leadership

While the in-depth process used by LifeLight begins with individual study and cannot achieve its aims without this individual effort, it cannot be completed by individual study alone. Therefore, trained leaders are necessary. You fill one or perhaps more of the important roles described below.

The Director

This person oversees the LifeLight program in a local center (which may be a congregation or a center operated by several neighboring congregations). The director

- serves as the parish LifeLight overall coordinator and leader;
- coordinates the scheduling of the LifeLight program;
- orders materials;
- convenes LifeLight leadership team meetings;
- develops publicity materials;
- recruits participants;
- maintains records and budgeting;
- assigns, with the leadership team, participants to small discussion groups;
- makes arrangements for facilities;
- communicates outreach opportunities to small-group leaders and to congregational boards;
- follows up on participants who leave the program.

The Assistant Director *(optional)*

This person may assist the director. Duties listed for the director may be assigned to the assistant director as mutually agreeable.

The Lecture Leader

This person prepares and delivers the lecture at the weekly assembly. **(Lesson material for the lecture leader begins on p. 9.)** The lecture leader

- prepares and presents the Bible study lecture to the large group;

- prepares worship activities (devotional thought, hymn, prayer), using resources in the study leaflet and leaders guide and possibly other, outside sources;

- helps the small-group discussion leaders to grow in understanding the content of the lessons;

- encourages prayer at weekly leadership team and discussion leaders meetings.

The Small-Group Coordinator *(optional; the director may fill this role)*

This person supervises and coordinates the work of the small-group discussion leaders. The small-group coordinator

- recruits with the leadership team the small-group discussion leaders;

- trains or arranges for training of the discussion leaders;

- assists the director and discussion leaders in follow-up and outreach;

- encourages the discussion leaders to contact absent group members;

- participates in the weekly leadership team and discussion leaders equipping meetings;

- provides ongoing training and support as needed.

The Small-Group Discussion Leaders

These people guide and facilitate discussion of LifeLight participants in the small groups. **(Lesson material for the small-group leaders begins on p. 59.)** There should be one discussion leader for every group of no more than 12 participants. The small-group discussion leaders are, perhaps, those individuals who are most important to the success of the program. They should, therefore, be chosen with special care and be equipped with skills needed to guide discussion and to foster a caring fellowship within the group. These discussion leaders

- prepare each week for the small-group discussion by using the study leaflet and small-group leaders guide section for that session **(see p. 59)**;

- read the enrichment magazine as a study supplement;

- guide and facilitate discussion in their small group;

- encourage and assist the discussion group in prayer;

- foster fellowship and mutual care within the discussion group;

- attend weekly discussion leaders training meetings.

Leadership Training

LifeLight leaders will meet weekly to review the previous week's work and plan the coming week. At this session, leaders can address concerns and prepare for the coming session. LifeLight is a 1½-hour program with no possibility for it to be taught in the one hour typically available on Sunday mornings. Some congregations, however, may want to use the Sunday morning Bible study hour for LifeLight preparation and leadership training. In such a meeting, the lecture leader and/or small-group coordinator may lead the discussion leaders through the coming week's lesson, reserving 5 or 10 minutes for problem solving or other group concerns.

While it requires intense effort, LifeLight has proven to bring great benefit to LifeLight participants. The effort put into this program, both by leaders and by participants, will be rewarding and profitable.

The LifeLight Weekly Schedule

Here is how LifeLight will work week by week:

1. Before session 1, each participant will receive the study leaflet for session 1 and the enrichment magazine for the course. The study leaflet contains worship resources (for use both in individual daily study and at the opening of the following week's assembly) and readings and study questions for five days. Challenge questions will lead those participants who have the time and desire a greater challenge into even deeper levels of study.

2. After the five days of individual study at home, participants will gather for a weekly assembly of all Life-Light participants. The assembly will begin with a brief period of worship (5 minutes). Participants will then join their assigned small discussion groups (of 12 or fewer, who will remain the same throughout the course), where they will go over the week's study questions together (55 minutes). Assembling together once again, participants will listen to a lecture presentation on the readings they have studied in the previous week and discussed in their small groups (20 minutes). After the lecture presentation, the director or another leader will distribute the study leaflet for the following week. Closing announcements and other necessary business may take another five minutes before dismissal.

In some places some small groups will not join the weekly assembly because of scheduling or other reasons. Such groups may meet at another time and place (perhaps in the home of one of the small group's members). They will follow the same schedule, but they may use a cassette tape to listen to the week's lecture presentation. The discussion leader will obtain the tape and leaflets from the director. A cassette tape version of the lecture is available for purchase from CPH (see your catalog). Or a congregation may record the lecture given by the lecture leader at the weekly assembly and duplicate it for use by other groups meeting later in the week.

3. On the day following the assembly, participants will review the preceding week's work by rereading the study leaflet they completed (and that they perhaps supplemented or corrected during the discussion in their small group) and by reading appropriate articles in the enrichment magazine.

Then the LifeLight weekly study process will begin all over again!

Recommended Resources for Genesis

Concordia Self-Study Bible, New International Version. St. Louis: Concordia Publishing House, 1986. Interpretive notes on each page form a running commentary on the text. The book includes cross-references, a 35,000-word concordance, full-color maps, charts, and time lines.

Delitzsch, Franz. *A New Commentary on Genesis.* 2 vols. Edinburgh: T. & T. Clark, 1899. A careful handling of theological issues in Genesis, making purposeful use of both Hebrew and Aramaic. A valuable resource.

Leupold, Herbert C. *Exposition of Genesis.* 2 vols. Grand Rapids: Baker Book House, 1942. This commentary is a careful exposition by a conservative scholar.

Luther, Martin. Lectures on Genesis. *Luther's Works.* 8 vols. Edited by Jaroslav Pelikan and Helmut T. Lehmann. St. Louis: Concordia Publishing House, 1958–70. Rather lengthy comments but patient, discerning reading of these volumes is rewarding.

Roehrs, Walter R., and Martin H. Franzmann. *Concordia Self-Study Commentary.* St. Louis: Concordia Publishing House, 1979. This one-volume commentary on the Bible contains 950 pages.

Every Voice a Song Pipe Organ Accompaniment for 180 Hymns and Liturgy. St. Louis: Concordia Publishing House Item #99-1565. Use this misic CD for worship hymn accompaniment.

The Line of Jacob Is Established

Genesis 25:12–28:22

Preparing for the Session

Central Focus

The influence a godly father can have on his son is awesome. One would assume from Isaac's previous history that his spiritual influence would have been great, but Esau's careless attitude and Jacob's deceitful character demonstrate that Isaac's will was weaker than his eyes. Thus, it would take the heavenly Father a great deal of time to mold Jacob into the spiritually influential patriarch he would become in his later years.

Objectives

That the participant, as a child of God and with the Holy Spirit's help, will be led to

1. observe the influence (for good or bad) that parents have on their children;

2. praise God for continuing the line of promise in ways beyond our expectations;

3. thank God for His continuing protection over our lives, even when we do not deserve it.

Note for small-group leaders: Lesson notes and other materials you will need begin on page 59.

For the Lecture Leader

This course continues the story of how God began His covenant line in Abraham and fulfilled His promises through Abraham's descendants. (Videotapes of the Genesis Project's New Media Bible may assist the LifeLight leadership team in bringing this continuity to life so that it may be taught to others.) This first session covers nearly four chapters, so it is important that the small-group leaders pace their discussion time. A brief summary of the basic highlights of the LifeLight course on the first half of Genesis may be helpful in establishing continuity for the small groups. If you have a number of participants who did not take part in the first LifeLight Genesis course, you may wish to use some of the introductory materials from the leaders guide of the previous course.

Chronicling the failings of great patriarchs such as Isaac and Jacob may not seem likely to impress some newer LifeLight participants to Scripture. But you may discover that exposing their shortcomings makes it easier for all of God's people to relate God's grace and mercy to their own lives, which also evidence failings and shortcomings.

Note: This course, unlike some of the other LifeLight courses, features a short devotional talk as part of the opening worship and a correspondingly shorter series of lecture presentations. Thus, you will want to schedule accordingly, beginning and ending the small-group discussion period five minutes later than usual.

Session Plan

Worship

Begin the session with the hymn and prayer printed in the study leaflet. Follow with the devotion. Hymn accompaniments are available in denominational hymnals, such as *Lutheran Worship* (refer to hymnal index).

Devotion

There is a story about Mr. Smith, a man who loved the neighborhood children and whose forgiving attitude toward even the worst of boys was amazing. One day Mr. Smith poured a new cement driveway, but after dark some mischievous boys found the fresh cement and "mistook" it for the front of Mann's Chinese Theater, leaving their shoe prints for posterity. When Mr. Smith discovered the damage the next morning, he blew his stack so loudly that the whole neighborhood could hear. Surprised by the outburst of such a gentle, fatherly figure, one of the neighbors approached him. Gazing at Mr. Smith standing on his new driveway, the neighbor said, "I thought you loved all children." Mr. Smith thought for a while and then replied, "I guess I love them in the *abstract*, but not in the *concrete*."

Experienced parents agree that raising children is not a job for the fainthearted, even though the dividends of good Christian parenting are eternal. Perhaps that is why Scripture mentions the words *child* and *children* nearly 2,000 times, reminding us that offspring truly are a heritage from the Lord.

Sadly, parents can emotionally scar that heritage by playing favorites. Comedian Tommy Smothers had a routine in which he insisted that Mom liked his brother, Dick, much better. "That's simply not true," claimed Dick. "Oh, yeah," responded Tommy, "then why was it when we asked to have a pet, Mom gave you the puppy and I got the chicken?"

Siblings very often feel that way about how their parents treat them. In today's LifeLight study Esau and Jacob, the treacherous twins, may have rightly felt that way about their parents, Isaac and Rebekah, who seemed oblivious to how their deceptive schemes would result in "splitting heirs."

What a blessing that our heavenly Father loves each of us with an impartial and caring love that numbers each hair of our head, as well as each heir of His promise. Christian parents, who know their heavenly Father, will never play one child against another. Instead, they will bring their children up in an atmosphere where love, peace, and harmony are not merely taught but lived out through their own parental example. God made us a family. We are privileged to share His love and forgiveness with each other.

Lecture Presentation

Introduction

Security. It is a prized commodity. We save; we invest; we buy insurance. We order our lives so that our future might be "secure." Yet, we're painfully aware that risks remain. A dramatic drop in the stock market can produce instant panic! How much security do you have? How can your future be more secure?

To answer these questions it is helpful to look at biblical characters. Sometimes they appear to be without hope. But then, suddenly and inexplicably, they enjoy security in full measure. Isaac and Jacob are perfect for this purpose. They lived when security was hard to find. There were no banks. There were no poverty programs. A famine … a drought … a raid—these could crush a family at any moment. Slavery could replace security. The prospect of an untimely death could replace prosperity. Isaac and Jacob were nomads. To feed and water their flocks and herds required movement, and movement exposed them to real dangers.

Yet, the patriarchs took pleasure especially in one area of their lives—their children. Our culture frequently views children as a burden or an obstacle to security. But the patriarchs viewed children as central and necessary for a full and secure life—not simply as security, but as great blessings!

1 The Line of Ishmael

For this reason Genesis details the many descendants of Abraham by Ishmael (Genesis 25:12–18). Far from merely rehearsing facts, Ishmael's genealogy alerts us to God's gracious hand in Abraham's history.

First, we see that God keeps His Word. God fulfilled His promise to Hagar (Genesis 16:10: "I will so increase your descendants that they will be too numerous to count"). God's plan of salvation includes many nations like the Ishmaelites.

Second, this genealogy shows that God's promise to Abraham (Genesis 12:1–3) was remarkably realized as his name is made great through his many descendants.

Finally, the short summary of Ishmael's children (Genesis 25:12–18), followed by the detailed description of Isaac's family, focuses our attention on the messianic line. We have already seen this pattern of prefacing the messianic line with nonmessianic lineages in chapters 4 and 10.

"This is the account of Abraham's son Ishmael… . This is the account of Abraham's son Isaac." Note that Genesis completes the career of Abraham with an account of his children, not with his bank account!

2 The Line of Isaac

Verses 20–22—This emphasis on children is also central in the description of Isaac's adult life. His marriage at the age of 40 is followed immediately by the crisis that remaining childless had created: "Isaac prayed to the LORD on behalf of his wife, because she was barren" (25:21). Isaac illustrates the familiar expression Like father, like son. The parallel begins in Rebekah's barrenness; it will continue in later events.

The atmosphere was clearly one of crisis. God responded by graciously answering Isaac's prayer. Rebekah became pregnant with twins.

Isaac and Rebekah are not simply wooden pieces that God moves across the checkerboard of history. Their hopes and anxieties are transparent. Their faith is intertwined with impatience. Like us, they both create and are caught by many problems. For example, Rebekah's pregnancy was not easy. She could feel the twins struggling within her. The conflict was so severe that Rebekah feared for her life. (Literally, the text in verse 22 reads, "Why do I live?") The Lord answered with a short summary of the future. The two sons would father two nations. Contrary to custom (25:5), the older would serve the younger (25:23).

Just as God had promised the birth and blessing of Isaac (Genesis 17:15–16), so the Lord of history foretold the lives of Esau and Jacob. By graphically describing their births, the text alerts us that even the first moments of life signaled what would come later. Esau's "hairy" or "red" appearance suggested a man of the outdoors. Jacob's grasp of Esau's heel provided a name that means

both "heel" and "deception." The suitability of these names will become obvious later. Even more evident will be God's hand in the history of Isaac's family.

Yet, the scene is not set in heaven. These are human beings whose behavior we recognize. The tensions in the family are described as frankly as the strife that had separated Sarah and Hagar (chapter 16). Isaac, due to his fondness for wild meat, favored Esau. Rebekah, on the other hand, preferred Jacob (25:28). We can easily imagine how these preferences displayed themselves in little ways day after day. Over a period of time the hurts hardened into hostility.

A key instance of such conflict is provided in verses 29–34. Verse 29—Esau returned from a hunt, famished. Verse 31—Jacob exploited Esau's hunger by requiring his birthright in exchange for some food—the very opposite of a brotherly attitude! Verse 33—An oath sealed the exchange. Oaths in antiquity were the equal of today's notarized, legal documents. This transaction, so far-reaching in its results, grew from dark motives. Jacob refused to share a simple meal without requiring Esau's forfeiture of his birthright. Esau, on the other hand, put his appetite ahead of his birthright.

Genesis, unlike the great epics of Egypt, tells the whole truth, even about its chief characters. We don't meet divine and perfect figures, such as the pharaohs portrayed by Egyptian scribes. Rather, we find ourselves in the center of a family fight. There is more here than moralism. The point is the very real presence of God in such sad situations. Then, and now, the promise and presence of God—the God of Abraham, Isaac, and Jacob—is with sinful men and women. God does not remove Himself from people with wrong motives.

This presence of God in the Old Testament anticipates the real presence of Christ among fallen humanity in the incarnation. The gracious patience of God with such people finds its precise parallel in His mercy upon us. Christ's coming removes any question that God's presence in the Old Testament was casual or conditional. Then, and now, His presence points to His purpose: the salvation of sinful people.

3 The Lifeline Is Threatened

"A few inches more … a few seconds more. It would all have been over!" Most of us have had a near miss. Perhaps it was on an interstate as a truck sped by. Perhaps it was at home as an alarm alerted us to danger. Whenever, in a sobering moment we sensed that our life was on the very brink of extinction. In less than a second our lives can be lost to the accidental and the unexpected. **You may wish to refer, instead, to a near miss in your own experience.**

Chapter 26 describes a slower but no less significant threat to Isaac's security. Verse 1—All he has is threatened by a famine. Water for his herds and food for his family: these were daily needs a nomad couldn't stockpile. Isaac went to reside with the Philistines. They inhabited the southwestern coast of Palestine and were known for their sailing skills. Probably these events occurred before the birth of Jacob and Esau. The famine description, including the loss of Esau's birthright, highlights God's investment in this history. What God had done so much to guarantee, Esau gives away for lentil stew (verse 34). The famine brought Isaac's household into contact with Abimelech, king of the Philistines. *Abimelech*, like *Pharaoh*, is a title, meaning "father is king." (An earlier king in Abraham's time—20:2—also bore this title.)

Verse 2—As the Lord had appeared to Abram (12:7), so He now appeared to Isaac with a specific warning not to go down to Egypt. The real point of this appearance is to restate the promise to Abram (vv. 3–4): "Stay in this land for a while, and I will be with you and will bless you. For to you and your descendants I will give all these lands and will confirm the oath I swore to your father Abraham. I will make your descendants as numerous as the stars in the sky and will give them all these lands, and through your offspring all nations on earth will be blessed."

Here is security no famine can threaten. Isaac and his family are safe. How? God's presence and promise guarantee the future. This security is offered to all in that child who would come from Abraham and Isaac's line—Jesus (Genesis 12:2–3; 13:16; 15:5). Verse 4—The remarkable truth is that through the offspring of a famine-fleeing Isaac "all nations on earth will be blessed."

The Gospel promise, like its fulfillment in Christ, is framed in people and places that none of us would expect. Our taste is for trumpets and fanfare. Our natural preferences are for established power and wealth rather than a fleeing desert prince. But the promise came then, and comes now, in God's own manner. Isaac's seemingly weak and tenuous existence bears a blessing for all. Christ crucified is the Savior of all!

The drama becomes even more engaging when that existence is threatened by more than a famine. From within Isaac, as from within Abram, came a more subtle and insidious danger: a lack of trust. The promise was sure. The future was secure. But Isaac worried about the present. He tried, like Abram, to safeguard his life with a lie. Verses 7–11 tell how Rebekah is represented as his sister for safety's sake.

Verse 10—The serious threat to Isaac's seed was perceived even by Abimelech: "What is this you have done to us? One of the men might well have slept with your wife, and you would have brought guilt upon us." As with us, the temptation to trust in our own plans rather than God's presence placed Isaac at risk. But God doesn't give up! He remains. Verse 11—In Isaac's case God protected Rebekah through the edict of the Philistine prince.

God does more than protect! He provides blessings! Verses 12–14 rehearse how lavishly and liberally Isaac was blessed. So great does Isaac's estate become that it brought about a crisis. The Philistines were envious of his prosperity. They sought to stop such growth by filling up the wells used by Isaac's flocks.

The pivotal place of water in antiquity again becomes obvious. Verses 16–17—Abimelech requested Isaac's departure, and the patriarch complied. The strife in Israel today, as well as battles over water rights in our own Southwest, is not new. Our situation and our dispositions are not superior to the ancients! Verse 22—Even as God provided room for Isaac's family to live in peace, His presence is the only security for 20th-century wanderers.

Chapter 26 closes with two episodes. Verses 23–25—First, God again appeared to reassure Isaac. This repetition of the promise reminded and refreshed Isaac. Verse 25—His natural response, like Abram's, was worship. Second, Abimelech approached with a request that a pact be made between them. Verse 28—His reason for approaching Isaac should not be missed: "We saw clearly that the LORD was with you." The Lord's presence is so transparent that even a Philistine prince can see it! The processes by which Isaac and Abimelech frame a treaty (oaths and public statements) are widely attested from this period.

Lest we see Isaac's world suddenly problem free, verse 35 concludes the chapter with an observation that Esau's Hittite wives grieved Isaac and Rebekah. It is likely that these women were continuing to practice their pagan religions. Esau, who so lightly regarded his birthright, was evidently equally lax in domestic matters.

4   The Pivotal Place of Blessing

If evidence is needed for God's presence, chapter 27 shows how completely God commits Himself to human beings. The context for Isaac's blessing displays the cunning and deception that our modern society also knows so well. Think how today's families can contest the last will and testament of a loved one. God's good gift of family can be changed from an oasis of love to a desert of strife. The great detail provided us points to the pivotal place of blessing in the world of the patriarchs. God's guidance attended the blessing of Isaac, like the later blessing of Jacob (Genesis 49). The blessing determined the future! Both parties in the dispute desperately wanted the blessing.

Both sides decided to take matters into their own hands. Verse 23—Isaac wanted Esau to receive the blessing despite the Lord's earlier oracle. Verses 15–17—Rebekah wanted Jacob to have the blessing, even at the price of deception. Neither was prepared to await the Lord's good pleasure in guiding events.

The result is now familiar to us. Instead of improving matters, the deterioration of family ties accelerated. The blessing was conferred upon Jacob. So severe was Esau's disappointment that he planned to kill Jacob. From twin brothers to the prospect of a Cain-like murder of Jacob, the rupture of the relationship is complete. Jacob had to flee all the way to his uncle Laban in Haran!

Several events show God's continued control and guidance. Verses 37–40—First, Isaac recognized the binding blessing he had bestowed on Jacob. Whether he did so because ancient custom forbade changing a blessing or because he sensed that God's will, not his own, had been done, the result was the same: Jacob was blessed! This change in disposition is confirmed by the manner in which Isaac recalled Jacob and repeated the blessing in Genesis 28:3–4. Isaac and Rebekah also admonished Jacob to take a wife from his kindred people. Verse 9—Aware that his parents were not pleased with his wives, Esau responded by taking an Israelite wife. He clearly hoped to reverse the situation. But, like an arrow once released, the blessing of Jacob cannot be retrieved!

5   Jacob's Remarkable Dream

Verse 10—The text next shifts our attention to Jacob's journey. Verses 13–15—We are transported in the desert night to Jacob's camp. The fact that his pillow was a stone reflects the ancient practice of sleeping on hard surfaces. Even the pharaohs used hard, sometimes metal, headrests for sleeping. The reason the text directs us to Jacob's camp, however, is the remarkable dream he has there. Here, far from the centers of power and in the dark of the night, God again rehearsed His great covenant promise. The dream, with its stairway to heaven, recalls the great stairways of ancient temples. The ascending and descending angels alerted Jacob that he was in the very presence of God.

Marking the place with a pillar and naming it Bethel (house of God) set it aside as a sacred site. But the real significance of this scene is the promise in verse 15: "I am with you and will watch over you wherever you go." Unlike pagan gods, who claimed jurisdiction only over a restricted area, the Lord assured Jacob of His abiding presence.

Alone in the desert night. Alienated from a brother. Exposed to the dangers of ancient travel. Jacob was still safe and secure. His safety was in God's presence. His future was in God's promise.

Now this is security that can be enjoyed. It will not evaporate with ill health or dissolve with a sick economy. It is sure; God guarantees it. The security we all seek is freely available in the presence of God. Jacob would see that truth in his many descendants. We have seen that truth in Jacob's greatest descendant, Jesus Christ: the one seed in which all the nations of the earth can have security and salvation.

Concluding Activities

Speak a prayer, asking God's blessing on participants in this LifeLight course and that God's Holy Spirit might enable all to grow in knowledge of and faith in God's plan for them. Then make any necessary announcements and distribute study leaflet 2.

Notes

Jacob's Marriage: The Line Flourishes

Genesis 29:1–31:21

Preparing for the Session

Central Focus

This lesson focuses on a family—a greedy, cunning, and deceptive family out of which God can still bring blessings and a Messiah.

Objectives

That the participant, as a child of God and with the Holy Spirit's help, will be led to

1. learn patience in the face of injustice;

2. praise God for always keeping His promises;

3. grow in integrity, especially when dealing with members of his or her own family;

4. rejoice in the blessings received by others.

Note for small-group leaders: Lesson notes and other materials you will need begin on page 62.

For the Lecture Leader

This lesson may seem like the script to a new soap opera entitled, "Greed, Deceit, and Other Family Matters." Nevertheless, God is still in control despite the attempts at one-upmanship we see in these chapters; His will still is accomplished. This lesson will provide many opportunities to address family relationships and how we are to treat one another as members of God's family. It also speaks to employer-employee relationships and the problem of injustice in this world. Although the main characters do not always set a shining example for us, we can learn from their mistakes. Furthermore, God uses the events in these chapters to mellow Jacob and begin reshaping him. We can ask God to do the same in our lives.

Session Plan

Worship

Begin the session with the hymn and prayer printed in the study leaflet. Follow with the devotion. Hymn accompaniments are available in denominational hymnals, such as *Lutheran Worship* (refer to hymnal index).

Devotion

There's a supposedly true story about a stingy man who kept his family in hand-me-downs but gave himself most anything he wanted. He also managed to salt away a sizable portion of his wages, which the family never saw. His saintly wife, in particular, endured this lifestyle throughout their marriage. Neighbors said that if anyone could find a way to beat the IRS and take it with him, this man could.

Stuffed inside the man's mattress was a considerable part of his life savings—$30,000 in small bills. As the miser lay dying, he made his wife swear she would put his savings into his coffin and bury it with him. Cruel and uncaring as this last wish sounded, his wife kept her word. The very day of her husband's death, she deposited the money into her bank account, wrote out a personal check for $30,000, and dutifully placed it into his casket!

Avarice has a way of turning back on ourselves, while generosity returns in overflowing measure. In this week's LifeLight study, Jacob, the deceiver, learns some lessons about the wages of sin from another greedy man. For that matter, so does Laban. Through the midst of the bargaining and labor contracts, Jacob experienced God's gracious hand of blessing. Wise as a serpent and almost as innocent as a dove, he dealt patiently with Laban, a worldly man who brought new meaning to the term *minimum* wage.

In the end, Jacob looked at his blessings and realized that he did not get what he deserved; he got more than he deserved—not of evil, but material blessings beyond measure and the spiritual blessings of God's continued presence in his life throughout adversity and injustice.

As God's people, we can expect to be used and abused by the fortune hunters of this world. Maybe that's not so bad. It makes us realize that our true fortunes are with God. God has balanced the scales of justice with His own Son, who was willing to pay the wages that none of us were willing to accept. Even beyond that, each day He blesses us with—to use Luther's words—"all that I need to support this body and life." Not to recognize that is to deceive ourselves. For all his faults, even Jacob, the deceiver, was not guilty of that.

Lecture Presentation

Introduction

The soap opera (or daytime drama). Have you ever watched one? Have you watched one recently? Do you watch one regularly? Market analysts say that millions do. Why do they appeal to so many people? If you are a fan, or even an infrequent viewer, what draws you to a soap opera?

One explanation, experts agree, is our endless interest in the human situation. Fame and fortune; fidelity and infidelity. Conceit and deceit; pride and power. From triumph to tragedy, we are simply fascinated by the variety of human emotions. The range of human feeling seems infinite.

1 A Meeting at the Well

Genesis 29–31 is far from a soap opera. There is nothing contrived about this plot! The characters are real, not artificial. Here all the emotions of human beings emerge in sharp focus. These feelings are intertwined with complex motives. The turns and twists of these three chapters are many. Betrayals, deceptions, jealousy, anxiety: they are all here. So are romantic love, a full life, and God's gracious blessing. If we read carefully and look closely, it won't take long to recognize these impulses and emotions in our own makeup. These men and women are children of Adam and Eve even as we are. They are not fairy-tale figures.

Chapter 29 begins with a scene that could be drawn from Lawrence of Arabia. Shepherds keep their flocks as they mill about at an oasis in the desert. Suddenly a stranger appears and asks questions. Jacob is clearly concerned about his situation. He is unfamiliar with the shepherds. Verse 5—He asks if they have heard of Laban. The setting is obviously charged with anxiety. If Jacob is thought to be a spy, he could be killed quickly. If he is seen as vulnerable, he could be made a slave.

Life and death issues were often decided near ancient wells. Access to water was essential to nomadic life. All would note the appearance of a stranger. In fact, to this day, certain wells still provide their precious commodity to nomadic peoples. Several thousand years has not altered this aspect of their life: all depends on adequate water for family and flocks!

Verses 5–6—Jacob seeks to locate Laban. Rachel's arrival conforms with the ancient practice of a daughter serving as a shepherdess. Verses 9–11—Rachel's spontaneous assistance, as well as the emotional greeting, might characterize any family reunion. Verses 12–14—Rachel runs to tell Laban. Laban runs to welcome Jacob. This immediate and total hospitality was considered central to nomadic life. It is still the case in much of the Near East today. A guest is given the best, and a relative is always welcomed heartily. To do otherwise would be a great affront to Semitic sensitivities.

2 For Love's Sake …

Verse 15—After a month, Laban raises the question of wages for Jacob's labor. This question provides an opportunity for Jacob. Verse 18—He proposes that he work seven years for Rachel's hand in marriage. His poverty requires him to earn the "bride-price" (Exodus 22:17). This payment to the father of the bride was to compensate for the loss of a daughter. It was viewed as an essential part of the marriage rite.

Verse 20—If we doubt the depth of affection in Jacob's heart, all we need to do is reflect on this sentence: "So Jacob served seven years to get Rachel, but they seemed like only a few days to him because of his love for her." Few men today would labor for seven years and feel they were "only a few days" for love's sake!

But, just as we find the height of human affection, we also encounter the depths of duplicity. Verse 23—Laban, at the last moment, substitutes Leah for Rachel! Various theories account for how such a switch could go unnoticed. Women were heavily veiled at weddings; perhaps a veil was in place. Several days of festivity with wine and song were also routine. Perhaps Jacob's senses were impaired. Verses 25–27—Whatever the reason, Jacob awoke with Leah. When Jacob protests, Laban appeals, somewhat lamely, to the custom of marrying the elder daughter first. While this custom was known in antiquity, it was hardly justification for such deception. Laban proposes that Rachel be given in marriage immediately after the bridal week. He also expects seven more years of labor. Laban's standing and wealth are clear in his presentation of Zilpah to be Leah's maid and Bilhah to be Rachel's maid.

As with Abraham's multiple mates (Sarah and Hagar), tension soon arises. Leah, not unexpectedly, is neglected. Verse 31—But the Lord "saw that Leah was not loved." The Lord's gracious presence blesses Leah with four sons in quick succession. Verses 32–35—Each son bears a significant name: *Reuben* means "see, a son" and sounds similar to the Hebrew for "he has seen my misery." *Simeon* means "[God] has heard." *Levi* means "attached." And *Judah* means "praise." **You may list on a chalkboard, transparency, or newsprint sheet Jacob's children as the names come up, together with the meaning of each name.**

These sons and their descendants figure prominently in Old Testament history. Levi founded the priestly line, which led to Aaron. Judah founded the royal line, which led to Jesus, the Messiah. Leah, the one not loved by her husband, is blessed beyond measure by her Maker. She is the ancestor of God's own Son! God uses the unwanted and insignificant to build His kingdom in the Old Testament as well as the New. Leah's place as mother of the Messiah is similar to Mary's, the handmaiden of the Lord.

Verse 1—Rachel's reaction reminds us that children were viewed as great gifts in the world of the patriarchs. She cries to Jacob, "Give me children, or I'll die!" Jacob becomes angry and shouts—verse 2, "Am I in the place of God, who has kept you from having children?" Pain.

Anger. Jealousy. All the contours of human feeling are well defined.

Rachel, like Sarah, seeks help in the ancient practice of providing a maid—Bilhah. Verses 6–8—When Dan is born, and later Naphtali, Rachel rejoices. They are counted as her children!

This jealous race between Leah and Rachel for more children leads to a remarkable episode. The mandrake plant was thought to induce pregnancy when eaten. When Reuben returns from the field, Rachel requests several of the mandrakes. Rachel offers Leah a night with Jacob in exchange for the mandrakes! The similarity with some soap operas becomes almost too close at this point!

Verses 18–21—God again heeds Leah's pleas for children. She bears Issachar ("reward"); Zebulun ("honor"); and a daughter, Dinah. Verses 22–24—This chronicle of birth concludes when Joseph is born to Rachel. Throughout the first section of this chapter, the longing for children carries the action forward.

3   Who Shall Have the Most?

From verse 25 forward, the longing for wealth, or the "love of money," motivates the actions. In this case the contest is not between Leah and Rachel, but between Laban and Jacob. Not children, but the number of sheep and goats is the measure of the full life!

Verse 26—The contest begins with Jacob's request to "Give me my wives and children, for whom I have served you, and I will be on my way." Laban's response is revealing. First, he pleads with Jacob to stay, not for affection's sake, nor for family reasons, but because Jacob has been good for Laban's business. Laban senses that Jacob's presence has brought blessings! Second, verse 27—we learn that he has resorted to divination for an answer. Laban discouraged Jacob's departure because of what he learned through magical means. This was Laban's guide. Later God would command that divination not occur in Israel (Leviticus 19:26; Deuteronomy 18:10–11). Laban, not unlike us, acknowledged the Lord's activity, but he stumbled by seeking a more secure word through divination. This apparent contradiction does not surprise us. Our old flesh and our faith daily struggle against one another.

What follows is a fascinating story of negotiation and struggle for possessions. Verses 31–34—Jacob opens the exchange with the overstatement: "Don't give me anything!" (v. 31). He quickly qualifies this suggestion with a request for "every speckled or spotted sheep, every dark-colored lamb and every spotted or speckled goat" (v. 32). Laban quickly agrees to what appear very good terms. Speckled or spotted sheep would have been of lesser value and of fewer numbers in ancient herds.

Verses 35–36—Laban loses no time in carrying out the provisions of the agreement. Verses 37–42—Jacob, through his own means of deception, promotes the growth of his flock in numbers and in quality. Jacob, like Abram (Genesis 12:1–3) and Isaac (Genesis 26:24), is blessed by Yahweh.

4 Big Business

The contrast between Jacob's increased wealth and Laban's lesser possessions leads to conflict! Chapter 31:2 states simply and eloquently how jealousy can change the human heart: "And Jacob noticed that Laban's attitude toward him was not what it had been." Verse 3—At this point, the Lord directly intervenes and instructs Jacob, "Go back to the land of your fathers."

Verses 15–19—The response of Rachel and Leah indicates that they too feel slighted. Laban had not treated them very well. The human contours in which God's will is realized become even clearer as Rachel steals Laban's household gods and Jacob secretly flees. Verses 22–55 describe Laban's pursuit of Jacob, their meeting, and the resulting conversations. Verses 27–28—Again we are exposed to the complexities of human emotion and motivation! Laban pleads that Jacob's secret flight has robbed him of the festivity and affection of a proper farewell. Verses 31–32—Laban also inquires about the whereabouts of his household gods. Jacob responds that he feared Laban would not let his daughters go, and he invites Laban to search for the gods. Verses 35–36—Rachel's cunning kept her secret. Since he did not know what Rachel had done, the search kindled Jacob's anger.

Human emotions lace chapters 29–31. Some are noble and honorable; others are quite the opposite. How marvelous that these emotions and actions—even the all-too-apparent deception, greed, and jealousy—do not obstruct God's gracious promise!

Perhaps soap operas are popular because they frequently show the way things are among the children of Adam and Eve. God's presence with such people, in Jacob's world and in ours, is a radiant witness to His mercy and grace. The fact that one of Jacob's descendants would be God Himself in human flesh is beyond our comprehension. Yet Scripture declares it is so! What comfort to know that God continues His gracious presence in Word and Sacrament despite the soap operas of our own sin!

Concluding Activities

Invite participants to speak a silent prayer, thanking God for the people who are most important in their own lives—spouse, children, parents, siblings, friends—and asking for God's help in maintaining these relationships in love and peace.

Then make any necessary announcements and distribute study leaflet 3.

Notes

Jacob's Confrontations: Tension on the Line

Genesis 31:22–33:20

Preparing for the Session

Central Focus

This lesson focuses on confrontation within the family of God—confrontation with a father-in-law, with a brother, and even with God Himself.

Objectives

That the participant, as a child of God and with the Holy Spirit's help, will be led to

1. see God's protective presence surrounding us at every moment;

2. experience the benefits of wrestling with God in prayer;

3. learn to confront our problems with God's help rather than to run away from them;

4. celebrate the joy of reconciliation.

Note for small-group leaders: Lesson notes and other materials you will need begin on page 65.

For the Lecture Leader

It seems that just as Jacob tries to escape one conflict, he is immediately confronted by another. All of us can relate to that. Jacob, who tended to live by his wits, learned the hard way that it would have been wiser to call upon God in prayer for His help before acting. Fortunately, God's gracious hand still was on Jacob as he moved closer to the Promised Land. Use this lesson to emphasize how God's hand is also on all of God's children, even in the midst of our confrontations with members of the family or when we tend to act before we pray.

Session Plan

Worship

Begin the session with the hymn and prayer printed in the study leaflet. Follow with the devotion. Hymn accompaniments are available in denominational hymnals, such as *Lutheran Worship* (refer to hymnal index).

Devotion

John Wesley (1703–1791), the founder of what became the Methodist church, spent 52 years in the saddle, preaching the Gospel to his generation. In those days the highways and byways were treacherous places to find one's self alone. Stagecoaches traveled with armed guards because bandits seemed to lurk behind every bush and tree. Gallows along the roadsides were common sights as reminders to holdup men of what would happen to them if they were caught.

One day John Wesley was riding his horse along a lonely stretch of highway when he noticed some shadowy figures ahead—forms that quickly disappeared behind a hedge almost as soon as he spotted them. It was not Wesley's style to turn and run in the face of danger. Yet, to go on could mean a possible mugging or even death! It was a long, deserted stretch of road with no help in sight, so Wesley prayed.

Almost at once he heard hoofbeats coming up behind him. He turned to see another traveler ride up alongside of him. After Wesley greeted his new traveling companion, the two silently proceeded down the road on past the place where the would-be robbers were hiding. Seeing two men instead of one, the thieves chose to let the men pass. Wesley then turned to say something to his companion, only to discover that there was no one there! The mysterious stranger had disappeared into thin air! Evidently, Wesley had experienced a supernatural glimpse of the angelic escort God sent to protect Wesley on his perilous journey.

Centuries before Wesley's time, the Old Testament patriarch Jacob also experienced the protection of angels. As a shepherd Jacob knew the importance of protecting his sheep from the dangers that threatened them. The Good Shepherd is even more caring and protective of His lambs. As Jacob faced a potentially lethal reunion with his estranged brother, Esau, we are told that he was met by a company of angels. Just as he had seen the angels ascending and descending at Bethel two decades earlier, God was reassuring Jacob of His presence to watch over him and to bring him back safely to the land He had promised.

And so God continues to keep His promises to the members of His flock today. Although we may not always be able to see the angelic escorts, they are there, doing the bidding of the Good Shepherd, who calls each of His lambs by name and surrounds them with His supernatural love and protection.

Lecture Presentation

Introduction

A great warship slowly approaches its home port. From every possible point officers and sailors look toward the dock. Wives, children, and friends appear as mere dots. Eyes search; hearts throb; emotions rise. The atmosphere is electric.

More frequently than civilians realize, this scene provides a setting for one of the most moving and joyous of all human experiences: a reunion with loved ones.

The train, the car, and especially the jet have made such reunions rare. A college student can attend classes on one coast and not miss a major holiday at home on the other coast! But, at least in segments of the military, separations are still common. Long deployments bring great pain. Dockside reunions bring the greatest joy! **You may substitute a homecoming or family reunion scene of your own or one that will be more familiar or more meaningful to your audience.**

1 A Family Reunion

Genesis 32 prepares us for the family reunion of chapter 33. In the ancient world long separations characterized many families. In some cases, slave markets sold members of the same family to masters from far-off places. The family members would never see each other again. This reunion is between brothers who had been apart for nearly 21 years. Their appearance, marital status, economic standing: all these had changed.

This reunion is different from a dockside homecoming. **Refer to your own homecoming/reunion scene if you make a substitution above.** It is full of anxiety and suspense! The parting of these brothers had been so painful. Jacob had fled from Esau to save his life (Genesis 27:41)! Had Esau's anger smoldered over the years? Had Jacob's deceptive acquisition of Isaac's blessing burned itself into Esau's memory? Would Esau, the rugged outdoorsman, now avenge himself (Genesis 25:27)? These questions raced through Jacob's mind.

God had told Jacob to return to Canaan (31:3). Yet, as Jacob approaches Esau's territory, his anxiety grows. Genesis 32:1–2—Angels appear to assure him of God's presence. Jacob had named the place where he had previously met with angels Bethel ("house of God"—Genesis 28:19). He now names this place Mahanaim ("two camps"). The name is appropriate. First, Jacob recognizes that God's camp is near his own. Second, he had just moved his camp from Laban's encampment. Finally, he was about to enter Esau's territory. Jacob's life literally is between "two camps"!

Yet the angels' presence does not take away Jacob's anxiety. Verses 3–5—As a precaution he sends messengers ahead to Esau. His grave concern is obvious. Jacob gives his men the exact wording they are to use in addressing Esau. They are to announce Jacob as Esau's "servant." They are to indicate that Jacob desires favor in Esau's eyes. This delicate breaking of the ice is designed to test Esau's mood. Is it safe to go on? Or is it suicidal?

Verses 6–7—The messengers return. Their message is ominous: Esau is approaching with 400 men! As Abram had taken 318 trained men to rescue Lot (Genesis 14:14), Esau now apparently will avenge himself with a similar unit of fighting men. Jacob is distraught! The text stresses his alarm, repeating that he was in "great fear and distress."

Verse 8—Jacob quickly divides his household into two camps. His strategy is desperate. While Esau is occupied with an attack on one camp, the other camp might escape. At least something will be left! As Abram had divided his forces to attack (Genesis 14:15), Jacob now divides his household so some might survive! Such a strategy was important in the nomadic world. Survival could not be assumed. Shrewd, speedy action was essential!

In this moment of greatest peril Jacob utters a beautiful prayer, one of the most profound prayers on the lips of any of the patriarchs. We might ask whether our prayers aren't at their best when our situation is at its worst? Aren't we much like Jacob? Jacob's prayer appeals to God's promise. Verse 12—Fearful that Esau's force will wipe out his whole family, Jacob cries to God, "But You have said, 'I will surely make you prosper and will make your descendants like the sand of the sea, which cannot be counted.' " This plea is preceded by a simple confession in verse 10: "I am unworthy of all the kindness and faithfulness You have shown Your servant." Jacob's prayer provides a perfect pattern for us: a confession followed by an appeal to God's gracious promise.

After a night's rest Jacob follows a delicate, diplomatic approach to Esau. He sets aside a gift of select animals. Verses 13–15—Goats, ewes, rams, camels, cows, bulls, donkeys: Jacob gathers a liberal number from each category of his livestock. The Hebrew word for gift also describes an offering of reconciliation to God. This gift is Jacob's effort at reconciliation with Esau.

Jacob again gives specific instructions to his servants. They are to meet Esau in three waves. At each point they are to repeat that these animals are a gift from Jacob (32:18). Verse 20—The motive is obvious. Jacob thought, "I will pacify him with these gifts I am sending on ahead; later, when I see him, perhaps he will receive me."

Note that Jacob doesn't march recklessly forward. He joins his faith to prudence. Today we might say that "he used his head." God's promise to care for us does not mean that we can live with abandon. Rather, we are called to use our "reason and senses."

2 An Unexpected and Mysterious Meeting

Verse 22—In this desperate situation, with Esau's approach bringing almost certain death, one of the most remarkable events in all the Old Testament occurs. Jacob moves his immediate family across the Jabbok River. This water course, or wadi, is about 20 miles north of the Dead Sea. Jacob is preparing to meet Esau. Instead, he meets a mysterious man. Verses 24–26—All night they are locked in a wrestling match. They struggle until daylight, but it is a standoff. Jacob's hip is dislocated, but he continues to cling to this mysterious man. Jacob will simply not let go until the man imparts a blessing!

Verse 28—The man responds by changing Jacob's name. "Your name will no longer be Jacob, but Israel, because you have struggled with God and with men and have overcome." Names were important in antiquity. A name was no mere label! A name, particularly one bestowed under such strange and mysterious circumstances, signaled a reality. Israel means "he who struggles with God."

In a manner beyond our understanding, this all-night contest had matched Jacob against God Himself! Jacob was aware that no one can see God as He is and live. Verse 30—In gratitude for his life, "Jacob called the place Peniel, saying, 'It is because I saw God face to face, and yet my life was spared.' " Probably the "man" with whom Jacob wrestled was the angel of the Lord, God Himself—a preincarnate manifestation of Christ. Abraham also had met the Lord as a "man" (Genesis 18).

The remarkable reality was that Jacob, now Israel, spent the night in God's presence. This closeness of God should not be missed. He was present. Such a presence with Jacob, as with us, is an experience of expansive grace. God, in the Old Testament, is not just at the top of Mount Sinai. He is also down in the Jabbok Valley with Jacob. He comes to spare Jacob's life.

The Israelites continued to remember this remarkable event in a special way. They would no longer eat a tendon attached to a hip socket—verse 32—"because the socket of Jacob's hip was touched near the tendon." This dietary practice acknowledged Jacob's (Israel's) God.

We may visit a restaurant for only one purpose—to satisfy our hunger. In ancient times the way one went about eating also expressed faith. Perhaps Christians parallel this by saying grace in a public restaurant. Not eating the tendon attached to the socket reminded the people of Israel to whom they belonged. They were the Lord's. By bowing our heads and folding our hands, we can be seen as a particular people. We are the Lord's.

3 A Fraternal Reunion

Chapter 33 begins on an ominous note. The moment had come. Esau is in sight. Jacob quickly divides his household (33:1). Leah, her maids, and her children were placed in front. In that action Jacob's greater love for Rachel shows itself. She and Joseph are located at the greatest distance from Esau, where there would be the best chance of escape! How human is this man who had wrestled all night with God.

Verse 3—Jacob goes before his company and bows down to the ground seven times. This custom denotes complete submission. Jacob wants Esau to recognize his approach as friendly. *But* … This one little word turns Jacob's world around. Verse 4—Instead of charging to attack, Esau runs to Jacob and embraces him! Affection pours out in tears and even kisses. To this day showing affection between male family members in this way is common in the Near East.

God reveals His guiding and saving presence in this unexpected reception. God—who had told Jacob, "Go!"—would also go with him. God's power could reverse Esau's red-hot anger.

Verses 6–8—A touching sequel follows. After the initial reunion, Jacob introduces his immediate family. Esau inquires about the meaning of the many presents. Jacob replies, "To find favor in your eyes, my lord" (v. 8). Again, Jacob expresses complete respect for Esau.

Verse 9—Demonstrating Near Eastern negotiation, Esau at first refuses the gift. All knew this was only a polite way to receive the gift. Jacob, also aware of that, insists. Now Esau is free to accept the gift—and he does. We would say, "Oh, you shouldn't have done this!" What we mean is that we are deeply appreciative. In the patriarchs' day a similar subtlety would be understood by all.

The chapter ends on a note of caution. The negotiating and posturing regarding the future are not over. Verse 12—Esau invites Jacob to return with him. But Jacob

pleads that his family, which includes children and young animals, would suffer great losses if they were to travel at the speed of Esau's band. Verses 17–20—After repeating his gratitude for Esau's favor, Jacob moves his family first to Succoth (literally "shelters") and then to Shechem, where he purchases land and builds an altar.

So Jacob has fled from Laban only to face Esau. There would seem to be no way out. But from God's perspective, Jacob was safe and secure. The angel of the Lord, who would later slay all the firstborn sons of Egypt, would not kill but would bless Jacob (32:26).

Genesis 33:4—Esau, so likely to slay Jacob, would surprise him with an embrace. All of this is not to show how "lucky" or "successful" Jacob was. No, these improbable, even impossible, turns of events point us to the greatest surprise of all: God's gracious presence with one as frail and human as Jacob.

Our lives, too, are sometimes caught between flight and fear—flight from God and fear of His punishment for our sin. But God surprises us. He runs to embrace us; He remains with us. More than that, He sends His Son to the cross that all fear might be gone. In Christ God's gracious presence is guaranteed.

Concluding Activities

Read (or have someone else read) Psalm 133. Following the psalm speak a brief prayer, thanking God for the unity we have in Christ and for the Christian harmony we enjoy.

Then make any necessary announcements and distribute study leaflet 4.

Notes

Jacob's Daughter: Violence on the Line

Genesis 34–36

Preparing for the Session

Central Focus

Jacob's life was a spiritual roller coaster. We sinners/saints can empathize with this great patriarch's spiritual highs and lows. The impact of Jacob's up-and-down spirituality on his family is the focus of this lesson.

Objectives

That the participant, as a child of God and with the Holy Spirit's help, will be led to

1. observe the influence parents have on shaping the morality of their children;
2. rejoice in forgiveness rather than wallow in revenge;
3. live a life free of the violence of sin;
4. affirm God's covenant grace, no matter what he or she has done.

Note for small-group leaders: Lesson notes and other materials you will need begin on page 68.

For the Lecture Leader

This lesson is not shy about revealing the character of God's people—warts and all. It begins with a chapter devoid of God's name or of any God-pleasing actions. However, it is followed by two chapters that affirm God's covenant with His fault-filled people. Despite the degenerate actions described in chapter 34 and the long lists of ancient names in chapter 36, a wealth of lecture and Bible study discussion material abounds in all three of the chapters encompassed in this lesson. Participants will benefit from tracing Jacob's movement in these chapters by referring to a map of Bible lands at the time of the patriarchs.

Session Plan

Worship

Begin the session with the hymn and prayer printed in the study leaflet. Follow with the devotion. Hymn accompaniments are available in denominational hymnals, such as *Lutheran Worship* (refer to hymnal index).

Devotion

There's a story about two brothers who vied with each other at Christmastime to see who could give their mother the most unusual present. One year Bill learned that Tom was giving a custom-built Cadillac. As Bill was passing a pet store, he saw a parrot with a price tag of $10,000. He asked the manager why there was such a fantastic price on the bird. He was told this was a very rare parrot that could speak 17 languages fluently.

Delighted, Bill purchased the bird and shipped it to his mother, convinced he had topped his brother for sure. He could hardly wait until Christmas Day to call her and see how she liked it. He said, "Mother, how did you like the bird?"

"It was delicious," she answered.

"Delicious!" he screamed. "Mother, that bird was rare. It cost me $10,000, and it speaks 17 *languages!*"

"Well, why didn't it say something before I put it into the oven?" replied his mother.

Why didn't it say something, indeed! One gets the same feeling about Jacob. God had a lot of time and grace invested in him. Then why didn't Jacob say something to Dinah when this teenager was allowed to go unescorted into a pagan town? Why didn't he say something to defend Dinah's honor or God's principles when impenitent Hamor and Shechem tried to buy him off? Why didn't he say something to his murderous sons about the slaughter of human life instead of merely being concerned about his reputation or what the neighbors might do?

In spite of God's investment in this patriarch, Jacob chose to remain silent and abrogate his responsibilities of spiritual leadership. Consequently, the foul stench he attributed to his sons' actions was really the smell of his own goose cooking.

At times we also find ourselves hesitating to speak up. We forget that God has invested an eternity of promises in us. He has also given us a faith in Christ equipped to speak boldly and fluently, even to people ready to ridicule that faith.

Lecture Presentation

Introduction

Violence. It is a word that makes us pause. It is a word we hear too often. It is, tragically, a word that accurately describes too many human actions.

Genesis reflects the same world we face. Chapter 4 holds before us the horror of the second man to walk this earth (Cain) killing the third man (his own brother Abel). The violence that marks our own culture has a long history, going back to the beginning of time!

1 A New Land, an Old Problem

Chapter 34 straightforwardly describes one of the worst forms of violence: rape. Jacob had just settled near Shechem. Verses 1–4—Dinah, a daughter born to Leah, visits the women of the land. The text is direct: "When Shechem son of Hamor the Hivite, the ruler of that area, saw her, he took her and violated her" (v. 2). Probably this man Shechem received his name from the city of the same name (Genesis 33:18). Since his father ruled the region, Shechem tells Hamor: "Get me this girl as my wife" (v. 4).

The pride and presumption of power are transparent: Shechem will take what he wants! We need not look far for the same practices among the powerful in our own day. Verse 5—But Jacob, the cunning brother of Esau and the consummate trader with Laban, will not con-

cede so easily! He remains silent while his sons are absent. To violate a virgin or another's wife (Genesis 20:9) was a horrible thing. It was an act that should not happen in Israel (Genesis 34:7)! When Dinah's brothers hear, they are filled with "grief and fury."

Verses 7–18—Following their father's lead, they feign negotiations for Dinah's hand in marriage. Hamor approaches Jacob. He offers Canaanite women as wives and free access to his land. Shechem also speaks, offering the brothers a blank check for the bridal gift (v. 12): "Make the price for the bride and the gift I am to bring as great as you like, and I'll pay whatever you ask me." Jacob's sons present what appears to be a counterproposal. If Hamor, Shechem, and all their men are circumcised, the marriage will be consummated. It appears to be a fair request.

Verses 20–23—Hamor and Shechem head straight to the city gate where such agreements were normally debated and decided. The men of the city are persuaded by Hamor and Shechem that they will gain Israel's livestock, property, and other animals. Both sides have a hidden agenda! Doesn't such positioning sound all too familiar to us? Motivated by greed, the men of Shechem proceed. Every male in the city is circumcised.

Verses 25–29—While the men of Shechem are still recovering, Simeon and Levi strike. They were sons of Leah—Dinah's full brothers. Their revenge is swift and vicious. Not only Hamor and Shechem, but every male is slain. The city is caught by surprise! This initial vengeance is followed by looting (vv. 28–29): "They seized their flocks and herds and donkeys and everything else of theirs in the city and out in the fields. They carried off all their wealth and all their women and children, taking as plunder everything in the houses."

This was precisely the fate Jacob had feared when he faced Esau. In this case, Jacob's sons had set the trap. Their utter destruction of the whole city appears out of proportion. The spiral of violence is hard to stop! Even Jacob is concerned that this violence will provoke a reaction among the surrounding peoples (v. 30): "We are few in number, and if they join forces against me and attack me, I and my household will be destroyed." The brothers answer their father with a smug superiority—

verse 31—"Should he have treated our sister like a prostitute?"

Genesis certainly tells it like it is. There is no hint of softening the harsh realities. A violated maiden … a treacherous plan … a citywide massacre: these forms of violence are part of a patriarch's world. They are, undeniably, a part of ours as well. Yet, God does not abandon such a violent world; He does not abandon us!

As chapter 34 closes, Jacob fears retaliation. Even in this distress, there is evidence of God's presence and providence. As Walter Roehrs aptly states:

> Jacob thought only of threats to their physical welfare. But intermarriage with *the inhabitants of the land* would have canaanized and baalized the seed of Abraham, making them unfit for God's purposes. His intervention again used the evil deeds of men to promote His plan. Events had taken such a turn as to make Jacob realize that he could no longer retain his property among the Shechemites. He was anxious to obey the directive to "go up to Bethel." (35:1) (Walter R. Roehrs, *Concordia Self-Study Commentary* [St. Louis: Concordia Publishing House, 1979], 48.)

2 The Patriarch at Home

Genesis 35:1—"Go up to Bethel and settle there, and build an altar there to God." These words come from God. They are specific. Bethel is the place where Jacob is to settle. He is to build an altar to God there.

This command brought back memories. Jacob had stopped at this place and named it Bethel on his flight from Esau (Genesis 28:10–22). As he now returns, Bethel becomes a sign that God has sustained him. It reminds him of his vow to worship only the Lord (Genesis 28:20–22). Jacob immediately instructs his household (35:2), "Get rid of the foreign gods you have with you."

This command might surprise us. What was Jacob's family doing with foreign gods? Why hadn't they forsaken such deities long ago? The world of the patriarchs,

it is important to recall, was very "religious." Each country, each city, even private families possessed and promoted their own gods. To acknowledge and to worship only one god would have seemed strange!

Perhaps it is still a peculiar posture! Cars and boats and other things, not inherently bad, can become deities when they are loved more than the true God. If we compare the beautifully carved deities of antiquity with the metal trinkets that are sometimes worshiped in our day, is it not obvious that modern idolatry is more sophisticated! Rather than thinking it primitive to worship many gods, we might be well served by reflection on our own culture and context. Our gods can be equally primitive!

Jacob's whole family responds to his instruction. They part with their deities and discard the earrings, which frequently carried the images of such deities.

Verse 5 provides another glimpse of the patriarch's world. People of the ancient Near East assumed that when two nations fought, their gods also did battle. The battle between humans on earth was paralleled by a contest between deities in the heavens above. The credit for the victory went to the deity of the winning side! This assumption shapes the response of the surrounding cities: "And the terror of God fell upon the towns all around them so that no one pursued them."

Jacob's fear of the surrounding peoples (34:30) turns out to be groundless. God's presence with Jacob had caused fear in those around him! Again, Jacob's survival is tied to his trust. In fact, even when he fails to trust, his survival is guaranteed by God.

Verses 6–7—Bethel becomes a resting place for Jacob. Here the patriarch constructs an altar and worships God. This "habit" should not be missed. Over and over the patriarchs worship. Worship is central to their confession of God. It remains central for ours.

Bethel also defines Jacob's life. Here God appeared to him on his flight from Esau. Verse 8—Here, Deborah, Rebekah's nurse dies and is buried. Here God repeats his great and glorious promise: verses 11–12—"I am God Almighty; be fruitful and increase in number. A nation and a community of nations will come from you, and kings will come from your body. The land I gave to Abraham and Isaac I also give to you, and I will give this land to your descendants after you." This is the heart of God's promise. From Jacob, as from Abram (12:3), nations and kings will come forth. Indeed, all the nations of the earth will be blessed in one King, the Messiah (12:3).

Jacob's response is grateful worship. He builds a memorial pillar and pours forth a drink offering. Pouring liquids on a pillar was viewed as a sacrifice of thanksgiving (Exodus 29:40).

3 The Death of Rachel and Last Days of Isaac

Shortly after departing from Bethel, Rachel dies in childbirth near Bethlehem (Ephrath). While Rachel's dying inclination is to name the boy "son of my trouble" (Ben-Oni), Jacob exercises the father's right and names him "son of my right hand" (Benjamin).

While the text doesn't dwell on Rachel's death, Jacob expresses his loss by setting up a pillar to mark Rachel's tomb. Archaeologists frequently uncover similar pillars and large stones. Unfortunately, none of those recovered to date have patriarchal names. But this is possible! A New Testament parallel is the discovery, in this century, of a stone at Caesarea with the name of Pontius Pilate on it.

As Jacob, now called Israel, moves on, we're alerted to a problem. Reuben, Israel's firstborn, is eager to assert his preeminence. Verse 22—He arrogantly sleeps with Bilhah, Israel's concubine. This act, like so many prideful grasps for power, results in less rather than more for Reuben. Jacob's deathbed blessing removes his privileges as firstborn (49:3–4)! The remainder of chapter 35 describes Jacob's standing in terms of his sons.

Verses 27–28—Jacob now comes full circle to Hebron. Here, reunited with his father, he shortly joins Esau in burying Isaac. This short description says a lot. Jacob's flight is over; he is back in his own land. Jacob's fear is over. Esau is reconciled. Jacob's world is together again. God has kept His promise.

Chapter 36 stands as a counterpoint to chapter 35. Here Esau's clan is described alongside of Jacob's family. Even as God had blessed Hagar and Ishmael (Genesis

25:12–18), He now blesses Esau. The scope of this blessing is again measured in terms of seed. Verses 10–14—Esau is the father of many. Verses 15–43—He is also wealthy and the founder of Edom. The genealogies of Genesis again make the point: God keeps His promises. In the flesh-and-blood fulfillment of these promises, we are taught to look forward to a flesh-and-blood Savior, who comes to live in our world. More than this, He comes to save that world!

Concluding Activities

Speak a brief litany in which you ask God to deliver you from the violence of others, the violence that erupts within ourselves, a forgetfulness of God's benefits, neglect of worship, hopelessness in times of grief, and other matters suggested by this week's lesson. Cue participants at the conclusion of each petition by saying, "In Your mercy," so the others may respond by saying, "Good Lord, deliver us."

Following the litany distribute study leaflet 5 and make any necessary announcements.

Notes

Joseph's Dreams: Hope on the Line

Genesis 37–38

Preparing for the Session

Central Focus

This lesson begins the final section of the Book of Genesis, explaining how Israel became a nation of people who ended up in Egypt. This particular lesson, however, focuses on the moral tragedies out of which hope for an entire nation would develop.

Objectives

That the participant, as a child of God and with the Holy Spirit's help, will be led to

1. become aware of the consequences of favoritism;

2. view any sin as slavery;

3. understand that the ends do not justify the means;

4. appreciate how God can turn the evil of man to His good purposes.

Note for small-group leaders: Lesson notes and other materials you will need begin on page 71.

For the Lecture Leader

These two chapters do little to enhance the image of a chosen people. Sins stand out boldly. Nevertheless, we grow spiritually, not only from learning what to do, but also from learning what not to do. Use this lesson to bring home God's grace even in the midst of our most heinous or morally objectionable sins.

Session Plan

Worship

Begin the session with the hymn and prayer printed in the study leaflet. Follow with the devotion. Hymn accompaniments are available in denominational hymnals, such as *Lutheran Worship* (refer to hymnal index).

Devotion

It is an interesting fact of history that in the ancient world a country's coins were not minted with today's preciseness and quality control. Precious metals were melted down, poured into a mold, and then pressed with the image of the nation's monarch. Such coins usually had soft, irregular edges. All you had to do to get extra gold or silver was to scrape the edges of coins and accumulate the shavings. When you gathered enough shavings, you could melt them down and have enough for an extra coin. This was such a common practice that the city-state of Athens passed more than 80 laws against trimming coins.

When St. Paul wrote in 1 Corinthians 9:27 about how he disciplined his body so he would not be *disqualified for* eternal life, the word he used was a Greek term meaning "failing a test" or "not meeting a standard." This term describes a coin that has been shaved down so much that no merchant would accept it.

That whittling process can be seen in the lives of Jacob and his sons. Jacob's moral indifference and self-concern did little to help the morality of his sons. By his blatant favoritism Jacob set the stage for the mercenary, callous attitude of brothers who rationalized the sale of their own sibling into slavery while purposefully breaking their father's heart. As if that were not enough, Judah's assimilation into Canaanite culture and his affair with Tamar carved away even more at the elements that set Jacob's offspring apart from their pagan neighbors.

Certainly, Abraham and the messianic line were never

in spiritually mint condition from the start. They were chosen—as we have been—solely by God's grace. But factors such as prosperity, indifference, greed, sexual immorality, and even proximity to pagans had a tendency to slowly shave away their distinctness as a people of God—a holy and *separate* people. Nevertheless, God was setting the stage for an eventual move away from those pagan influences.

So also with us. We face such threats every day. But God's promise to us is secure as He qualifies us in Christ to be shaped, molded, and stamped into the image of God and His precepts for our lives.

Lecture Presentation

Introduction

Pecking order. Perhaps no problem is more persistent than this one! Who is first? Who is foremost? These questions come naturally to the children of Adam and Eve. Our ancestors asked them. We ask them today.

Who is first? This question permeates Genesis. Cain was jealous of Abel; Sarah of Hagar; Jacob of Esau; Rachel of Leah. Genesis also describes the pain that comes to all when pecking order becomes the chief question.

1 Who Is Dressed the Best?

Chapter 37 illustrates the perpetual nature of this problem. Verse 1 opens with the observation that Jacob lived "in the land where his father had stayed, the land of Canaan." **You may wish to point out Hebron on a map.**

This short verse says a lot. The land had been a part of the promise to Abram (12:1–3, 7). It had been a part of the promise to Isaac (Genesis 26:24; 28:13). It is now the place where Jacob lives. The ancient reader would take note. More is being described than Jacob's location. God, it would be noted, had kept His promise! The land was Jacob's!

God's good gift of land should have brought about the good life. There was pasture for the flocks. The land would provide all of life's necessities. But Jacob's family is torn by the problem of pecking order! Verse 2 intro-

duces the tension. Joseph brings a bad report about his brothers' behavior. Probably Jacob relied on Joseph for these reports. Or Joseph may have served the tattletale role voluntarily. Either explanation sets the stage for problems.

Verses 3–4 further heighten the tension. Israel's (Jacob's) greater love for Joseph shows itself in the gift of a richly ornamented robe. The potential for offense is immense! In the ancient Near East, the main robe was worn constantly. Every day the brothers would behold Joseph's superior garment. More than this, the main robe denoted status. One could determine pecking order at a glance! The costliest garment meant the most prominent person. Isn't the world of modern fashion similar?

Verses 4–8—The result is predictable. The brothers hate Joseph and "could not speak a kind word to him" (v.4). Joseph seems insensitive to the situation. When he dreams that he will be first among the 12, he doesn't hesitate to share the dream! A second dream adds insult to injury from the brothers' perspective. In this dream, his father and mother also bow down to Joseph! Since Rachel, Joseph's mother, was dead at the time, this dream may have occurred earlier in Joseph's life. In any event, Joseph eagerly repeats it to all. It appears that Joseph enjoyed his special status. He was foremost and wanted all to know it!

While we might discuss such a dream as arrogant fancy, Joseph's family would view it as a claim of God's plan. As Genesis has already shown, God used dreams (Genesis 20:3). Dreams were seen as one means through which God communicated His will. So Joseph's dreams pack a hard punch! The brothers get the message. They hate him "all the more" (37:8).

2 The Fruit of Jealousy: Fratricide

Verses 12–13—Hatred and jealousy are a potent combination. The stage is set. The brothers strike back. It happens at Shechem. **Again, you may wish to point to Shechem on a large map.**

The brothers are grazing the herd there. Jacob sends Joseph to check on their welfare. Joseph's insensitivity becomes even more evident! He is eager to go! Either ignorant of his brother's hatred or unconcerned about it, Joseph sets out. When Joseph arrives at Shechem, he learns that his brothers have gone on to Dothan, a city some 13 miles north. **Again—the map.**

The movement of nomadic peoples is again obvious. The need for fresh grazing areas drives a nomadic tribe over great expanses of land. It also exposes them to new dangers. Jacob's concern about his sons is justified!

Verses 19–20—As Joseph catches up with his brothers, their pent-up hatred propels them into action. Their bitterness is transparent. They say to one another, "Here comes that dreamer!" (v. 19). They will see to it that Joseph's dreams will not come to pass! They will kill him and say that he was devoured by a "ferocious animal" (v. 20). No chance will then remain that Joseph will rule over them!

Verses 22–24—Reuben, perhaps sensitive to his responsibility as the firstborn, tries to protect Joseph from death. The brothers quickly strip the richly ornamented robe from Joseph. No longer will his robe suggest a superior status! They then throw him into a dry cistern. These cisterns collected water in the rainy season for later use. After the water was used, the cavity would remain dry until the next rainy season. Many of these cisterns still exist today.

Verse 25—The brothers celebrate with a meal. As they are eating, a caravan of Ishmaelites approaches. Ancient trade routes crisscrossed Canaan, which occupied a strategic place between Egypt and the great civilizations of the Persian Gulf. Archaeology has confirmed that commerce flourished during this period. Spices, balm, myrrh, and many other goods would be transported by camels for quick sale and big profits.

Verses 26–28—Judah has an idea. Why not make some money from these merchants? Judah suggests selling Joseph rather than slaying him, for he is their own "flesh and blood" (v. 27). Throughout the ancient world, this point was weighty. Family bonds were guides to behavior. Blood mattered! Hence, Judah is reluctant to kill Joseph and "cover up his blood" (v. 26). Joseph is sold to the Midianite merchants for 20 shekels of silver. Trade in slaves was as profitable as the sale of perfumes!

When Reuben returns and can't find Joseph, he tears his clothing. His earlier concern for Joseph (verses 21–22) now expresses itself in the standard act of mourning, tearing one's garment. Jacob responds in the same way when his sons present Joseph's bloodied robe. Verses 34–35—"Then Jacob tore his clothes, put on sackcloth and mourned for his son many days." Jacob's suffering is severe.

Verse 36—The chapter closes with the simple observation that Joseph is sold in Egypt "to Potiphar, one of Pharaoh's officials, the captain of the guard." This summary sentence reminds the reader that Joseph is still alive. It also prepares us for later chapters in Joseph's life.

3 Judah and Tamar: The Fruit of Folly

"Why did he do that?" "How stupid!" Such sentiments could describe many modern actions. Men and women do things that are simply folly. Genesis describes the same sort of men and women. Chapter 38 holds before us the fruit of folly.

Verses 1–2—Events are set in motion when Judah marries a Canaanite woman. The concerns of Abraham and Isaac that their sons not marry Canaanite women is noticeably absent! The religious and ethnic wholeness of Israel is under constant pressure. God's people could vanish by absorption into surrounding peoples! Three sons are born to Judah and the daughter of Shua: Er, Onan, and Shelah. These same names have been found on ancient texts from this period, though no one suggests that they designate these same biblical characters.

Er marries Tamar. When God puts Er to death for his wickedness, Judah tells Onan in verse 8 to "fulfill your duty to her as a brother-in-law." Judah's order illustrates the practice of levirate, or literally, "brother-in-law," marriage. The essence of this practice was that a brother was under obligation to a deceased brother. If the brother had not begotten children, the living brother was to beget children by his sister-in-law. The offspring would legally be considered the children of the dead brother.

This might seem strange or even immoral from our modern perspective. Yet, it is important to recall the harsh realities of a nomadic culture. Men, on average, lived less than 30 years. There was no social security system. A widow was without any means of support. The brother-in-law, in such circumstances, brings support and hope to the widow. Verse 9—In fact, this is the very thing Onan refuses to do. For refusing his duty, Onan, too, is put to death by God.

Verse 11—Judah urges Tamar to wait until his third son, Shelah, grows up. Verse 14—Tamar notices, however, that Judah does not follow through on his promise. Tamar, now desperate, devises her own plan to have the "brother-in-law" duty carried out. She disguises herself and takes a position along the roadside.

Virtuous women avoided these public settings by quickly passing on their way. For a woman to linger suggested that she was less than virtuous. As Judah passes, he infers that she is a prostitute. Verses 16–18—His less-than-virtuous invitation is, "Come now, let me sleep with you" (v. 16). Tamar negotiates a price. Judah offers to send "a young goat from my flock" (v. 17). Tamar shrewdly asks for some pledge of future payment. When Judah asks what she would like, she requests his seal with its cord and his staff. These were unmistakable marks of his identity. The seal was used to mark items. The staff was a personal item. Both would be recognized as Judah's and no one else's. Tamar then sleeps with Judah and becomes pregnant.

Again Genesis tells it like it is. There is not a hint that the author is presenting only the positive side of these two characters. Judah and Tamar appear all too human! Verses 24–26—This point is underscored when the report of Tamar's pregnancy reaches Judah. Judah is indignant and demands the death penalty. Though this penalty was widespread (Leviticus 21:9), Judah's hypocrisy is exposed. Tamar presents his seal, cord, and staff. Judah suddenly sees his own guilt: " 'She is more righteous than I, since I wouldn't give her to my son Shelah.' And he did not sleep with her again" (v. 26). The birth of twin boys concludes the chapter. This unusual birth results in one being named Perez ("breaking out") and the other Zerah ("scarlet").

This whole sequence of events seems unsavory. It would be easy to think that God's plan had been thwarted by

human folly. But, in the midst of such matters, God displays His gracious presence. Perez fathers the leading clan in Judah. He becomes the ancestor of David (Ruth 4:18–22). He thereby also becomes the father of the Messiah (Matthew 1:1–16)! The messianic line, God's lifeline, continues. The folly of sin cannot cut the line! The frailty of human flesh cannot end it!

The obvious faults of Judah and Tamar should not cause us to throw up our hands in disgust. Rather, we should fold our hands in grateful prayer. There is enough of Judah and Tamar in each of us. But, God does not abandon us! His gracious presence remains. This gracious presence is proven by the birth of His Son. God's Son is born into a family line that includes Judah and Tamar. This line is God's lifeline to the whole human race. Christ's presence in our lives is the greatest proof of God's grace!

Concluding Activities

Form a "lifeline" or human chain by having participants join hands, with the presenter at the beginning of the line. The presenter speaks a brief prayer, thanking God for His promise to save us by sending a Savior. Then the presenter squeezes the hand of the person next in line, who adds a prayer. The squeeze is passed along the line until it is received by the person at the end. That person then also speaks a prayer, thanking God for keeping His promise by giving Jesus to be our Savior.

Make any necessary announcements and distribute study leaflet 6.

Notes

Joseph's Temptations: The Line at Pharaoh's Court

Genesis 39–41

Preparing for the Session

Central Focus

This lesson focuses on temptation—in particular, the temptation to seek revenge for past injustices.

Objectives

That the participant, as a child of God and with the Holy Spirit's help, will be led to

1. learn how blessings can come in the midst of trials;

2. see any sin as a sin against God;

3. find ways to serve God under all circumstances;

4. glorify God in times we are tempted to glorify ourselves;

5. let God pursue justice for us in His own time;

6. rely for strength in time of temptation on Jesus, our great High Priest, "who has been tempted in every way, just as we are—yet was without sin" (Hebrews 4:15).

Note for small-group leaders: Lesson notes and other materials you will need begin on page 74.

For the Lecture Leader

Because this lesson is about the temptations Joseph faced, it may be worthwhile to point out that leaders should not be tempted to read out loud to their groups the various cross-references in this lesson. Doing this would never allow the groups to finish the lesson in the allotted discussion time.

Encourage the participants to do their daily lessons each day and not at the last minute, so that they have time to meditate on the insights God's Word can bring to them.

Session Plan

Worship

Begin the session with the hymn and prayer printed in the study leaflet. Follow with the devotion. Hymn accompaniments are available in denominational hymnals, such as *Lutheran Worship* (refer to hymnal index).

Devotion

In some ways, the late Corrie ten Boom stands out as a modern-day Joseph. She and her sister, Betsie, were placed in Ravensbrueck, a Nazi concentration camp, for hiding Jews in their home during World War II. But her greatest test actually came several years after her release. Listen to her story:

> It was in a church in Munich that I saw him— a balding, heavyset man in a gray overcoat, a brown felt hat clutched between his hands. People were filing out of the basement room where I had just spoken, moving along the rows of wooden chairs to the door at the rear. It was 1947 and I had come from my home in Holland to defeated Germany with the message that God forgives ... I had told them that when we confess our sins, God casts those sins into the deepest ocean and then posts a NO FISHING ALLOWED sign.
>
> That's when I saw him, working his way forward against the others. One moment I saw the overcoat and the brown hat; the next, a blue uniform and a visored cap with its skull and crossbones. It came back with a rush ... the shame of walking naked past this man. I could see my sister's frail form ahead of me, ribs sharp beneath the parchment skin.
>
> "You mentioned Ravensbrueck in your talk," he was saying. "I was a guard there. But since that time ... I have become a Christian.

I know that God has forgiven me for the cruel things I did there, but I would like to hear it from your lips as well. Fraulein,"—again the hand came out—"will you forgive me?" [My sister Betsie had died in that place—could he erase her slow, terrible death simply for the asking?]

It could not have been many seconds … but to me it seemed hours as I wrestled with the most difficult thing I had ever had to do.

And so woodenly, mechanically, I thrust my hand into the one stretched out to me. And as I did, an incredible thing took place. The current started in my shoulder, raced down my arm, sprang into our joined hands. And then this healing warmth seemed to flood my whole being, bringing tears to my eyes. "I forgive you, brother!" I cried. "With all my heart."

For a long moment we grasped each other's hand, the former guard and the former prisoner. I had never known God's love so intensely as I did then, but even so, I realized that it was not my love. I had tried and did not have the power. It was the power of the Holy Spirit, as recorded in Romans 5:5 ("because the love of God is shed abroad in our hearts by the Holy Spirit which is given unto us").

Like Corrie ten Boom, Joseph, who had gone from prison to palace, had to learn to forgive, including his former master, Potiphar. It is a difficult yet wonderful lesson for all of us, to forgive others as Christ has forgiven us.

Lecture Presentation

Introduction

"What a character!" This expression easily comes to mind when we meet someone unique. Mannerisms, patterns of speech, or the sheer energy of someone's personality can impress us. Here is someone special!

In one sense, each of us is special. Even nonreligious people marvel over this remarkable truth: each of us is different from every other human being. Even look-alikes don't act alike! Even brothers and sisters can be dramatically different! Genesis describes the same differences in people that we experience today. Jacob and Esau were twin brothers. But Esau was an outdoorsman. Rugged and an avid hunter, he was the favorite of his father. Jacob, on the other hand, was a "man of the tent." Reserved and retiring, he was the favorite of his mother (Genesis 25:27–28). Brothers can be that different! They can be as different as night and day! **You may have examples right in your LifeLight group! Of course you will want to be careful about how you point out these examples.**

1 From Judah to Joseph: Counterpoint in Context

Genesis 39 describes such a sharp difference. Joseph acts in an entirely different manner than does his brother Judah! The contrast between the character of Judah in chapter 38 and that of Joseph in chapter 39 is sharp. This episode in Joseph's life is well known. Verses 2–6—Joseph rises fast in Egypt. Sold into Potiphar's service, the Lord blesses all that he does. Even an Egyptian prince could recognize that the Lord was with Joseph!

Verses 7–10—In such splendid circumstances, a serious problem arises. Potiphar's wife calls to Joseph, "Come to bed with me!" (v. 7). Joseph's response is a model of resistance. He sees the temptation immediately and strives to avoid it. " 'How then could I do such a wicked thing and sin against God?' And though she spoke to Joseph day after day, he refused to go to bed with her or even be with her" (vv. 9–10). Joseph knows that God sees even those sins done in secret (Psalm 90:8). The contrast with Judah's eager embrace of sin is complete and clear-cut.

But Joseph's virtue does not deliver him from difficulty! Genesis repeatedly locates the children of God in situations we can recognize. To follow God's will does not guarantee immediate deliverance and happiness. It frequently means suffering. The one who said, "Take up your cross and follow Me," also led the Old Testament saints through trouble. To follow the Lord, to be Christ's disciple, means to walk by faith, not by sight.

Verses 11–18—Joseph's life pointedly illustrates this truth. He did the "right" thing. The "right" thing got him into real trouble. One day Potiphar's wife physically grabs Joseph. His flight leaves her with his cloak in her hand. This cloak becomes her means for revenge. The household servants and then her husband are shown the cloak. The cloak is used as proof of Joseph's wicked action! Potiphar's response is predictable. Joseph is thrown into prison.

Verses 20–23—But that is not the end of Joseph! Rather, the text repeats, "The LORD was with him [Joseph]." Even in prison, the Lord gave Joseph success in whatever he did. Significant also is the note that he was with the king's prisoners. God positions Joseph for future service!

God's presence with us, in Christ, is no different. Whether our career is stellar or stale, God is for us and with us in Christ. If God is for us, who can be against us? Joseph cannot sin against God even if prison results. In prison God is for Joseph and with Joseph. The real presence of Christ in Word and Sacrament, whether in a palace or a prison, means God is for us and with us.

2 From Palace to Prison: Two Careers Crash

A Porsche is parked outside. The splash of water resounds from the swimming pool. The windows reveal expanses of elegantly appointed interior. Most of us don't live in houses like that! Perhaps some of us dream about such a home! But, even if we could construct our dream estate, it would still fall short of the splendor of Pharaoh's palace! The pharaoh, by law, owned the entire country. All its inhabitants, by law, were his servants. Their lives were completely subject to his will. Freedom as we know it would be foreign to their thinking.

Pharaoh and his palace were the religious, social, and political center of the nation. Everything revolved around Pharaoh and his court! To put Pharaoh's prestige in modern terms, imagine the religious weight of Rome, the political might of Washington, D.C., and the economic importance of the New York Stock Exchange all in one location! Pharaoh's palace was such a place.

In this setting, to work in or near Pharaoh was to be at the nerve center of the whole society. Positions here could bring the abundant life for good service or speedy death for some mistake. No positions in the palace complex were more precarious than those nearest the pharaoh. Perhaps the most delicate of all were those positions near Pharaoh's table!

In antiquity, poisoning was a favorite method of assassination. There were no forensic laboratories to determine the cause of death! Frequently the one serving Pharaoh's beverage first had to drink from it. Similarly, the one serving food had to sample it. It was a simple precaution against poisoning.

Chapter 40 takes us to the inner courts of Pharaoh's palace. We are brought to Pharaoh's private chambers. It is here that the one who was thought to be divine did the human tasks of eating and drinking. The cupbearer and the baker are crucial members of Pharaoh's staff. We're not told why, but they have fallen from Pharaoh's favor. They are sent from the palace to prison. From the center of wealth and power to a prison cell—they have moved from the highest to the lowest location within Egyptian culture.

Ancient prisons were far from pleasant. The Pharaohs used slaves for many of the projects. Slaves were a high percentage of the population. Most Americans and Canadians have never been in a prison. Nor have they seen a slave in person! It would have been hard to travel far in ancient Egypt without encountering both slaves and prisons. Verse 3—These servants and Joseph meet in prison.

Verses 6–7—As Joseph greets them at the beginning of the day, he notes that they look worried. "Why are your faces so sad today?" Joseph asks (v. 7). The answer is revealing. Dreams! Both servants have had strange dreams! They are puzzled and fearful. What could these dreams mean?

The servants' attitude reminds us that dreams were seen as divine media. God spoke through them. Just as Joseph's dreams disturbed his brothers, these dreams unsettle the servants. Joseph quickly asserts, verse 8—"Do not interpretations belong to God?"

Joseph is a good example of lifestyle evangelism. He notices the servants' demeanor, cares about them, engages them in conversation, and takes the opportunity to speak for God.

Verses 9–15—The remainder of the chapter demonstrates how interpretations do indeed "belong to God." First, the wine steward tells his dream to Joseph. Joseph immediately interprets it and adds a simple request, "Remember me" (v. 14). The wine steward's return to Pharaoh's side will provide an opportunity for Joseph. He cites the injustice of his imprisonment. He wants out of prison!

Verses 18–19—The chief baker sees an opportunity for himself. He now seeks an interpretation of his dream. He tells his dream to Joseph. Joseph also interprets it on the spot. But, tragically, the chief baker's dream denotes his death. In the original Hebrew, there is a play on the words "lift up your head." Joseph speaks the same phrase to both prisoners (verses 13 and 19). The phrase can mean "show favor to" or "grant a request," and it does mean this in the case of the cupbearer. However, in the case of the baker, the phrase was fulfilled literally; Pharaoh beheaded him. Verse 22—Three days later, it all happens "just as Joseph had said."

Two features of these events are noteworthy. First, the unqualified authority of an ancient monarch is obvious. He could end a life with a single word. Second, the complete reliability of Joseph's word is clear. Earlier, verse 8, he had asked the rhetorical question: "Do not interpretations belong to God?" Joseph gives God the credit. In the palace and in prison, Joseph lives "before God." It is against God whom he would sin in chapter 39. It is from God that his interpretation of dreams derives in chapter 40. We might think that such faith would make things "all right" for Joseph overnight. The last verse of the chapter, verse 23, speaks a soft "Not so." The chief cupbearer did not remember Joseph; he forgot him.

God's ways with Joseph (and with us!) are not so mechanical. He sees the whole picture. Our view is partial. Joseph awaits God's timing for deliverance. We too must wait.

3 The Great Reversal

Two years pass. The chief cupbearer forgot Joseph. "Has God also forgotten me?" This question must have crossed Joseph's mind many times. Then a simple event happens that would reverse Joseph's life. It would also deliver the nation Israel from a terrible famine. This simple event is a dream. Pharaoh has a dream in two parts.

Verses 2–8—First, seven fat cows are devoured by seven lean cows. Then, seven healthy heads of grain are swallowed by seven thin heads of grain. These mysterious actions unsettle Pharaoh. He, like Nebuchadnezzar much later (Daniel 2), does the standard thing: he calls his wise men and magicians for an interpretation.

None of the royal court can render an interpretation. A crisis situation is upon them. Pharaoh's every want and wish must be met! They could all die due to Pharaoh's frustration. In such a situation the chief cupbearer remembers Joseph. Verses 9–13—He recounts to Pharaoh how Joseph had helped him with his own dream in prison. The key point in the cupbearer's description is clear (v. 13): "And things turned out exactly as he interpreted them to us."

The hand of God is not mentioned in this sequence of events. But it is obviously and everywhere present. It is God who restores the chief cupbearer. It is God who causes Pharaoh to dream. It is God who remembers Joseph!

Joseph's life quickly reverses. He is summoned from prison to the palace. In accord with Egyptian protocol, Joseph is shaved and groomed. To approach Pharaoh improperly could bring instant death. It is noteworthy that, in Israel, a beard was viewed with pride. Shaving denoted mourning. In Egypt it was important to be clean shaven. Verses 15–16—Pharaoh immediately asks for an interpretation. Joseph shows his character once more: " 'I cannot do it,' Joseph replied to Pharaoh, 'but God will give Pharaoh the answer he desires.' " The hand of God is made explicit by Joseph. It is God who controls the history of men. It is God who will give Pharaoh the answer.

Verses 17–40—Pharaoh repeats his dream to Joseph. Joseph immediately interprets the dream for "God has revealed to Pharaoh what He is about to do" (v. 25). The dreams are fully expounded. Seven abundant years will be followed by seven years of severe famine. The two forms of the dream mean that God had firmly decided on the matter. It would most certainly happen. Joseph quickly offers a strategy to store food before the famine. Pharaoh is struck with Joseph's plan. He places Joseph at his side. Joseph is suddenly second in command in the world's greatest power. This position of "vizier" is well known from other Egyptian texts.

Verses 42–45—Chapter 41 concludes with a description of Joseph's new life. Pharaoh gives Joseph his signet ring. Like the seal of the president of the United States, this ring signified Pharaoh's authority and backing. A golden chain and a royal chariot complete Joseph's outfitting for high office. Pharaoh also gives Joseph an Egyptian name, Zaphenath-Paneah. The meaning of this name is uncertain. The fact that Pharaoh bestowed it, however, confers more status upon Joseph. Finally, Pharaoh provides a wife, Asenath, for Joseph. Joseph moves, by marriage, from the lowest "slave" class to the highest "priestly" class. To Asenath and Joseph are born Manasseh (meaning "forget") and Ephraim (meaning "twice fruitful"). Judah's earlier marriage to a Canaanite (chapter 38) is followed by Joseph's marriage to an Egyptian. Foreign blood mingles with Israel's blood.

Verses 53–57—These events happen during the seven years of abundance. When the seven years of famine begin, Joseph becomes the man of the hour beyond Egypt as well, controlling much of the world's food supply. "All the countries came to Egypt to buy grain from Joseph, because the famine was severe in all the world" (v. 57). God's hand had brought a solitary man from prison to Pharaoh's palace. God's hand now brings nations to that same man.

God's hand saves Joseph. It will now save a whole nation. More than this, it will save the lifeline—that people who will bear the Christ, the light of the world.

Concluding Activities

Read Psalm 130. If participants have the same translation of the Bible, the psalm can be read in unison. If not, one person can read the psalm. Or, a different person may read each verse, with everyone following along in his or her own Bible. If translations vary, so much the better, since this will give the psalm a special flavor.

Then make any necessary announcements and distribute study leaflet 7.

Notes

Joseph's Brothers: Reunion of the Line

Genesis 42–44

Preparing for the Session

Central Focus

This lesson centers on the spiritual refining process that God used, via Joseph, to set the stage for a long-overdue family reunion.

Objectives

That the participant, as a child of God and with the Holy Spirit's help, will be led to

1. recognize that sin will always find us out;

2. appreciate the processes God uses to change our hearts and bring us to repentance;

3. learn how to love those who have offended us and treated us unjustly;

4. see God's hand in bringing together estranged members of His family.

Note for small-group leaders: Lesson notes and other materials you will need begin on page 77.

For the Lecture Leader

We might read these chapters and see Joseph as a manipulator, controlling his brothers like a puppeteer and receiving sheer delight in the process. Therefore, it is important to assist your groups in seeing the refining nature of what Joseph was trying to accomplish by bringing his brothers to the point of true repentance— the point at which Joseph could then reveal his identity to them.

Session Plan

Worship

Begin the session with the hymn and prayer printed in the study leaflet. Follow with the devotion. Hymn accompaniments are available in denominational hymnals, such as *Lutheran Worship* (refer to hymnal index).

Devotion

A man troubled by his guilt attempted to put his conscience to rest. He wrote to the Internal Revenue Service, "I have cheated the government on my income tax and haven't had one good night of sleep ever since. Enclosed find my check for one hundred dollars. ... If I still can't sleep, I'll send you the balance."

Ever since 1811 the government of the United States has received self-imposed fines or guilt offerings from anonymous but troubled souls who had purposely shortchanged the government. Today, this "conscience fund" totals millions of dollars.

In this week's study we see how God makes good use of conscience in the lives of Joseph's brothers. Through a series of divinely orchestrated events, the little spark of conscience begins to burn brighter inside the hearts of these men until a surprising spark of human decency emerges from the flames.

The old adage of "letting our conscience be our guide" often doesn't work, for the voice of conscience can be muffled. In the case of Joseph's brothers, their corporate conscience had been dulled to the point of selling their brother down the river—the River Nile, that is. Their conscience went into a two-decade hibernation, occasionally tossing and turning in its troubled sleep, until awakened by circumstances beyond its control.

Ultimately, there is an answer to the troubled conscience. Hebrews 9:14 gives us that answer when it says, "How much more, then, will the blood of Christ ... cleanse our consciences from acts that lead to death, so that we may serve the living God!"

As Joseph—not in revenge, but in love—manipulated his brothers in order to test their character, he found them growing spiritually. Such an attitude adjustment comes only through true repentance that throws itself on the mercy seat of God.

No amount of money we pump into a "conscience fund" can buy peace of mind. Only the holy, innocent blood of Christ can pay such a price and soothe the conscience. Have you experienced that peace? The process is simple. Just come to the Lord as you are, willing to *admit* your sins rather than *hide* them. Only when we are willing to *come* clean will our consciences *become* clean.

Lecture Presentation

Introduction

Famine. Hunger. We hear these words. We know what they mean. Vivid images of famished people appear on our television sets. **If a famine has recently made news, you may wish to refer to it.** But, for most of us, our knowledge is a matter of the mind. We may have missed a meal. We've probably even said, "I'm starved!" Few of us, however, have gone for long periods without food! Our stomachs have not experienced hunger in this way. Our knowledge is of a different sort than those people who have survived a famine.

1 The Lifeline Threatened

Ancient people and nations frequently experienced famine firsthand. Abram had gone to Egypt for food long ago (Genesis 12). Now Jacob sends his sons to Egypt for grain (Genesis 42). The situation is serious. "Go down there and buy some [grain] for us, so that we may live and not die" (42:2).

The world of the patriarchs was not picture-postcard perfect! To romanticize their world misses the point of Genesis. They lived in the same fallen world we inhabit. If nuclear warfare poses a threat to much of our planet's life, they too faced such threats. This famine is literally a matter of life and death. The risks in going to Egypt were many. The alternative is even more menacing: certain death. Jacob, sensitive to the risk, sends all of his sons but Benjamin. Unaware that Joseph is alive, Jacob wants his only son by Rachel to remain with him (42:4).

2 A Remarkable Meeting

The God who fixed the galaxies in the sky can also place a single man in position. Joseph was now in place. All nations were coming to him to buy grain. Joseph controlled the food supply for that part of the world. His brothers come. And what a meeting it is! "So when Joseph's brothers arrived, they bowed down to him with their faces to the ground" (42:6). Joseph's dreams literally had come true (Genesis 37)! The brothers, though ignorant of Joseph's identity, were bowing down to him.

This meeting is remarkable. Since Egyptian royalty had a distinctive type of clothing and grooming, the brothers view Joseph as an Egyptian. In addition, he had grown to manhood over the years. They did not recognize him. Joseph, on the other hand, recognizes them immediately.

Verses 9–13—On this meeting hinges the whole future. Will Joseph take revenge? Will the brothers discover his identity? What will happen? Joseph appears hostile. He suggests that they are spies. It appears that Joseph is going to get even. In Egypt, as in most ancient cultures, a spy was subject to instant execution. A mere nod of the head would bring an end to the brothers! What will Joseph do? The brothers protest their innocence. They describe their family and share the fact that Benjamin is back with Jacob. They also tell Joseph that one brother "is no more" (v. 13). The irony of this meeting is overwhelming. The brother who "is no more" is actually before them.

Verses 14–16—Joseph quickly sets forth a strategy, demanding that their story be verified. They are to go and return with Benjamin. Joseph underscores this requirement with the phrase "as surely as Pharaoh lives" (v. 16). Rather than swearing by one of the Egyptian deities, Joseph calls on the prestige of Pharaoh. Joseph's faith remains in the God of Abram, Isaac, and Jacob! The brothers are held in custody for three days. They have little choice: death at the hands of the Egyptian or a return trip to bring Benjamin. Joseph further requires that one of them remain in Egypt as a guarantee they will return. The brothers quickly comply.

Verses 21–23—But, as they begin their return, they discuss their predicament. They connect their situation to Joseph's plight. Joseph had pleaded for his life. Now they must do the same! They now feel for Joseph, for they are in a similar situation.

If they only knew that they were pleading their case before the one whom they now remember! The drama of this encounter grows even more striking. The brothers openly discuss their sin against Joseph with the assumption that the Egyptian doesn't understand. Joseph understands every word! "They did not realize that Joseph could understand them, since he was using an interpreter."

Joseph is overcome by their words. He turns away and weeps! If we were writing a novel, the plot could hardly surpass this sequence of events. How clearly Joseph's humanity shows forth in his tears. Here is no robot. Here is a man overcome with emotion.

After regaining his composure, Joseph has Simeon bound and sends the others on their way. They go, unaware that Joseph knows exactly who they are. Joseph has ordered the servants to plant the silver payment in the brothers' grain bags. Verse 28—He intentionally raises the anxiety level of his brothers. They are terrified when the silver is discovered. "Their hearts sank and they turned to each other trembling and said, 'What is this that God has done to us?' " To be caught in thievery also meant certain death. The brothers could now be charged with two capital crimes!

Verses 29–38—Disturbed and distraught, they tell everything to Jacob. Jacob resists releasing Benjamin. Simeon and Joseph are lost. He will not lose Benjamin as well! Reuben offers his own sons to Jacob as security. If Reuben doesn't return home with Benjamin and Simeon, his own two sons are in Jacob's hand. But, Jacob will not budge! He will not risk the loss of another son.

This episode illustrates how important family ties were to the patriarchs. Their children were the center of their lives, their chief pride and pleasure. Perhaps our culture has gone backward in its frequent inclination to view children as obstacles to success and fulfillment.

So, the chapter ends on a note of crisis! Joseph is "no more." Simeon is in prison. Jacob refuses to send Benjamin. Things are at an impasse. Once again the human situation seems impossible. The famine threatens what is left of Jacob's family. The end of the family—the end of their lifeline—seems very near.

3 The Crisis Deepens

Famine. When it comes, it touches everyone. When it stays, its power is felt by all. Its grip permits no escape! Jacob's determination to keep Benjamin in Canaan is no match for famine's grip. Verse 2—The food from Egypt runs out. Without food, there is no future. Jacob's family, his entire family, will simply die. Jacob finally faces this harsh truth. He gives the order: "Go back and buy us a little more food."

Verse 5—Judah now speaks for his brothers. Without Benjamin, they will not go back! Behind their firm stand is the fact that they would face almost certain death if they displeased the monarch.

Jacob finally concedes that there is no alternative. The famine will not relent. Verse 11—His family's only hope is in "the man." He instructs his sons to take delicacies in addition to a double portion of silver. These products (balm, myrrh) and delicacies (honey, pistachios, almonds) were not native to Egypt. They were valued there. They might influence "the man." The irony of Jacob's instruction is immense. He seeks to influence "the man." "The man," of course, is his own son Joseph.

God's hand moves mysteriously among men. Neither Jacob nor Joseph is fully aware of what is happening. As readers we are invited to view God's gracious guidance. Both these men, we can see, will later recognize the blessing and benefit of God's presence. His hand is guiding events.

But, to appreciate this text, we must also walk with the brothers to Egypt a second time, not knowing what we might face. Verses 16–18—As the brothers approach, Joseph spots Benjamin. He instructs his steward to bring the brothers to his home for a meal. The brothers are suspicious: "We were brought here because of the silver that was put back into our sacks the first time. He wants to attack us and overpower us and seize us as slaves and take our donkeys" (v. 18).

The brothers fear a setup. The silver was planted in their sacks. The Egyptian will use the silver as sufficient cause to execute them! Verses 19–24—They quickly engage Joseph's steward to explain the sequence of events. They have brought that silver and more back for the Egyptian prince! The steward—undoubtedly at Joseph's instruction—calms their fears. The steward then brings Simeon out to them. He provides for them and their animals.

Verses 26–30—When Joseph arrives, the brothers bow down again. The poignancy of this action is obvious. Joseph's dream is fulfilled a second time! Joseph's plan, however, encounters a hitch. When he sees Benjamin, his composure melts. He hurries to his private chambers and weeps. Joseph's humanity and love of family are transparent. Reunion, not revenge, is what he longs for.

A lavish banquet follows. As was the custom in the land, the Egyptians and their guests eat in separate groups. Other ancient peoples practiced the same sort of hospitality. To eat with foreigners was to cross the lines of proper protocol.

4 The Silver Cup: Joseph's Strategy

The brothers must have enjoyed the banquet. The bounty of Joseph's table would contrast sharply with the famine provisions in Canaan. As morning dawns, they depart with full stomachs and full bags of grain. Their spirits must have been high.

Verses 6–12—Little do they know that in Benjamin's sack there is a silver cup planted by Joseph's steward. The cup would permit Joseph to recall Benjamin. The culprit who took the silver cup must stay behind. The strategy works perfectly. At Joseph's instruction, the steward overtakes the brothers, conducts a search, and discovers the cup in Benjamin's sack.

Verses 13–14—The brothers are distraught. They tear their robes. They return with Benjamin. For the third time the brothers bow down to Joseph.

Verse 15—Joseph places even more pressure on them

with several questions: "What is this you have done? Don't you know that a man like me can find things out by divination?"

Judah concedes that their situation is hopeless. How can they explain the silver cup? Judah offers that they all become slaves. Again, the irony is overwhelming. Those who had sold Joseph into slavery now offer themselves to him as slaves. They will bow down to him for life. Verse 17—But Joseph wants to keep only Benjamin, his full brother.

This move places Judah in a real predicament. How can he return to Jacob without Benjamin? He had given Jacob every assurance that they would return with Benjamin (43:8–9). Judah comes before Joseph (44:18), rehearsing in detail Jacob's delicate disposition.

Verse 33—Jacob will die if Benjamin does not return! Desperately Judah pleads for Benjamin's release and finally offers himself as a substitute: "Now then, please let your servant remain here as my lord's slave in place of the boy, and let the boy return with his brothers." The crisis escalates to this critical point. It appears that all is lost. Only Joseph and the reader sense that there is a way out.

God's deliverance often comes when it appears that there is no way out! One would come forth from Judah. This one would pray: "My Father, if it is possible, may this cup be taken from Me. Yet not as I will, but as You will" (Matthew 26:39). This one, Jesus of Nazareth, the Messiah, did as God willed. He drank the cup dry. For Judah, for Joseph, for us, Jesus has provided a "way out." This one's life, death, and resurrection were already present in God's promise to Abram, Isaac, and Jacob. We, with Judah and Joseph, can trust in the one who is "the way and the truth and the life" (John 14:6).

Concluding Activities

Close by telling your audience that there will be a moment of quiet for personal reflection and confession of sins they may have committed that day—or of sins from longer ago that continue to trouble them. End the period of silence by reading—or having someone else read—Hebrews 10:17, introducing the verse by saying: "This is what God says."

Make any necessary announcements and distribute study leaflet 8.

....

Notes

Joseph's Justice: God's Guidance of the Line

Genesis 45:1–47:12

Preparing for the Session

Central Focus

This lesson focuses on how God guided circumstances to finally bring about a reunion that healed the wounds left by sin and created a new episode in the history of God's people.

Objectives

That the participant, as a child of God and with the Holy Spirit's help, will be led to

1. value forgiveness;

2. understand that God has a plan for his or her life;

3. learn the importance of caring for the needs of one's family;

4. recognize the need to consult God for guidance before acting.

Note for small-group leaders: Lesson notes and other materials you will need begin on page 80.

For the Lecture Leader

Reunions can be emotional experiences. To set the stage for the events of this LifeLight lesson, you may want to share with your group a particularly moving homecoming or reunion experience.

Session Plan

Worship

Begin the session with the hymn and prayer printed in the study leaflet. Follow with the devotion. Hymn accompaniments are available in denominational hymnals, such as *Lutheran Worship* (refer to hymnal index).

Devotion

Read Genesis 45:7: [Joseph said,] "But God sent me ahead of you to preserve for you a remnant on earth and to save your lives by a great deliverance."

The oriental culture and its people have a reputation for being *inscrutable*, a word which dictionaries define as "mysterious, impenetrable, unfathomable to investigation."

This word seems especially suited to the Egyptian character. Just stand before the colossal carving of Ramses II at the great temple of Abu Simbel. Stare into that massive stone face and ask, "What is Ramses thinking? What is he feeling?" But there is no answer behind that cold face of stone—not even a clue. Even more inscrutable is the statue of the mysterious sphinx, not far from modern Cairo. The meaning of that great stone face has puzzled visitors to Egypt for centuries.

It is said that when you live in a place long enough, you tend to become like it. That must have happened to Joseph, at least in part. When we read about his dealings with his brothers before he revealed his identity to them, we find that more than two decades of life in Egypt had taught him to hide his feelings well, so that his own brothers did not suspect his true identity.

Yet, inside of Joseph was a Hebrew used to expressing deep feelings. Not surprisingly, then, we find Joseph on one occasion after another venting those deep emotions with private tears until, *in time,* his brothers, his servants, and the whole household of Pharaoh saw the depth of his great love and the forgiveness behind this inscrutable countenance.

So also with God. We often find Him inscrutable and wonder what He may be feeling about us and what His mysterious plans are for us. Certainly for many years, as Joseph languished in prison, he must have wondered also. But, *in time,* God revealed His plan, and Joseph recognized it as a plan to save the world and, in particular, God's covenant people.

In moments of despair or confusion, we may find God's ways inscrutable. We wonder if He feels anything at all for us. But, *in time*, His ways become clear, and we see not a cold, stone-faced idol, but a warm and caring God who, as St. Paul says, "When the *time* had fully come, … sent His Son … to redeem those under law" (Galatians 4:4–5, emphasis added). This was the Son who wept for his friend Lazarus and for the city of Jerusalem, and who forgave even those who nailed Him to a cross.

In time the inscrutable Joseph revealed himself in love and forgiveness to his family. *In time* God continues to do the same for us through His Son, Jesus Christ.

Lecture Presentation

Introduction

A doctor leaves surgery and enters the waiting room. All eyes are riveted on him; every ear is attentive. The whole family waits for his words. Has the accident taken their daughter and sister? Or has she survived? It seems like forever, but finally the physician utters three simple words, "She'll be okay."

A great sigh of relief bursts forth! Tears flow! Arms embrace! Anxiety is replaced by anticipation: "When can we see her?" "When can we talk to her?" To welcome back a family member in such circumstances is a profound joy. **If you have a similar experience of your own, relate it as an opening for the lecture.**

Even more frequently than accidents, jealousy and sin separate family members. The pain and sense of loss can be just as severe when strife divides a family unit. "I'll never talk to you again!" "I don't want to ever see you again!" How piercing and painful such statements are. Psychologists suggest that they can be more devastating to human beings than news of an accidental death. Yet, when reconciliation comes, it can have the same profound effect as the doctor's words *she'll be okay.* Life is suddenly brighter. Love replaces resentment. Laughter resounds. The hurt is healed. Genesis 45 describes a family reunion of this kind.

1 God's Family: Rift and Reconciliation

Judah's desperate pleas had concluded chapter 44. His situation seemed hopeless. He simply could not return to Jacob without Benjamin. The Egyptian prince would not budge. Judah and his brothers seem doomed. Their previous sin against their brother had brought this misery on them (Genesis 37). Judah and the brothers will die in an Egyptian prison. Jacob and those in Canaan will die by famine. This fracture in their family would now bring it to a tragic end! In this extreme and dire moment, the text suggests that something is about to break: Verses 1–9—"Then Joseph could no longer control himself" (v. 1). Joseph, overcome with emotion, orders his Egyptian attendants outside. "I am Joseph!" (v. 3). How these three words must have startled the brothers! Joseph reveals his identity in their own language! He asks about Jacob. The brothers are terrified. Their guilt brings fear to the heart. Joseph sees their fear and assures them, "So then, it was not you who sent me here, but God" (v. 8). Over and over he stresses God's hand in their action.

Forgiveness is fully and freely bestowed. Joseph looks beyond his brothers' frailty. He sees God's good and gracious hand at work. As one scholar has so aptly written: "The designs of wicked men, the weakness of His faltering saints, private plots and international barriers—none of these was able to frustrate the execution of His plan of salvation" (Walter R. Roehrs, *Concordia Self-Study Commentary* [St. Louis: Concordia Publishing House, 1979], 54). Verses 9–11—Joseph's forgiveness is genuine. He restores the family bond. He invites all of them to live in Goshen, the choicest part of Egypt.

Verses 12–15—Joseph's joy is transparent: "You can see for yourselves, and so can my brother Benjamin, that it is really I who am speaking to you. Tell my father about all the honor accorded me in Egypt and about everything you have seen. And bring my father down here quickly" (vv.12–13). The embrace—first of Benjamin, and then of all the brothers—seals the reconciliation. Not death, but a kiss, is bestowed.

To this day, men in the Arab world exchange kisses on the cheeks as an expression of friendship. What seems strange to American culture was standard practice in the ancient world. Sentiment was expressed by Semitic men. The weeping of Joseph flows from the same world. This weeping is like the sighs of relief in an emergency room.

Joseph's whole family has been restored. God's hand has moved in mysterious ways. The same hand now moves Pharaoh's heart. Verses 16–20—Pharaoh hears about Joseph's brothers and is pleased they have come. He orders the Egyptians to help Joseph's family relocate.

This hospitality would not have been the normal response of an ancient monarch. To settle a foreign people invited certain risks. But Pharaoh is a portion of God's larger plan of salvation for this people. His will can only serve God's will.

From famine and the threat of extinction, the brothers are now the beneficiaries of Pharaoh's pleasure! The best that Egypt has to offer is theirs. Provisions, new clothing, 20 donkeys with gifts and grain: all of these are theirs.

Verses 26–28—They return to Jacob to relate the events, telling him about Joseph. Such a reversal and reunion seemed impossible! Jacob is stunned! He doesn't believe their report! The concluding verse of chapter 45 completes the family reunion: "And Israel said, 'I'm convinced! My son Joseph is still alive. I will go and see him before I die.' " What a reversal. What a reunion! What a restoration!

2   The Great Journey

Verse 1—Jacob sets out for Egypt "with all that was his." This journey recalls others. Abraham had traveled this route. Isaac had come this way as well. Jacob pauses at the same place his father and grandfather had stopped: Beersheba. He, like them, worships there (Genesis 21:33; Genesis 26:23–25). Beersheba was a key crossroads on ancient trade routes. Its chief asset was its water. Archaeologists have uncovered a well at the site, which was there during Jacob's life.

Here, at this historic place, God speaks in a vision to Jacob. God appears to Jacob as he had to Abraham (Genesis 22:1) and to Isaac (Genesis 26:24). Verses

3–4—God identifies Himself as the "God of your father" (v. 3). God also gives Jacob a threefold promise: He will be with Jacob; He will make him a great nation; and He will bring him back to Canaan.

This promise parallels the one given to Abram (Genesis 12:1–3) and to Isaac (Genesis 26:24). It is the promise that his family will endure. It is the promise that the lifeline will go on. It is the promise that the Messiah, the seed of Abram, will be born.

This journey encompasses past, present, and future. It recalls Abraham's and Isaac's travels. It places Jacob's family beyond the grip of the famine. It provides a great future for Jacob's offspring. They will be a great nation (Genesis 46:3). So important is the survival of this family that the text draws our attention to its members repeatedly. Verses 7–26—We are told that Jacob took "sons and grandsons and his daughters and granddaughters—all his offspring" (v. 7). Then the entire family is named. Finally, the text provides a precise number for "all those who went to Egypt with Jacob—those who were his direct descendants, not counting his sons' wives" (v. 26). The count, including the two sons born to Joseph in Egypt, is 70. Again we see the importance of the family bond in Israel!

For Abram, Isaac, and now Jacob, neither peers nor careers were the center of their lives. Family, particularly children, were the most significant measure of their "success." The participants described history in terms of their family. No national or international calendar could serve them adequately.

It was the birth of Isaac that saved Abram from viewing his life as a failure (Genesis 15:1–6). In the births of Jacob and Esau, Isaac took great pleasure. And now, as they leave for Egypt, the family of Jacob must be described in detail. Armies could march. Great nations and kings could rise and fall. Genesis doesn't mention them. Genesis measures time by God's promise. This promise came to a nomadic family in Canaan. It was the promise that their family would not cease until the seed of the woman, the Messiah, was born.

Jacob's family was not the most powerful in the land, nor was it the most numerous. But God was with them. God appeared to them and not to the mighty kings of the major powers (Genesis 46:2). God's ways are recognizable. Later His angel appears not to the emperor, but to a young maiden. He appears not in Rome, but in Nazareth. This angel announces the birth of Jacob's Son. The birth of that Son would come to measure the history of humankind. So these long lists of names are not incidental. They are not filler for the story. They are central. God has delivered His promise to this people.

3 The Journey Continues

The reunion of the family is completed in Goshen. Verses 28–30—Judah goes ahead to get directions. The simplicity and elegance of the text's description cannot be surpassed: "Joseph had his chariot made ready and went to Goshen to meet his father Israel. As soon as Joseph appeared before him, he threw his arms around his father and wept for a long time. Israel said to Joseph, 'Now I am ready to die, since I have seen for myself that you are still alive' " (vv. 29–30).

The years of separation are past. Jacob sees that death has not claimed his son. He also sees that hatred has not fractured his family. Not unlike the surgeon coming to a family with good news, God has come to Jacob with proof that His promises have been kept. Just when all seemed hopeless, God sets everything right. Verse 30—Jacob (Israel) is so assured by Joseph's presence that he is prepared to depart to God in peace.

Joseph now advises his family on protocol before Pharaoh. Verses 33–34—They are to stress their status as shepherds. The Egyptians were farmers. They detested shepherds. This fact would set the stage for settling in Goshen. Again, we see how God uses men and women to accomplish His mission. Joseph's knowledge of Pharaoh's court serves the settlement of God's people. Jacob's family will receive the best real estate in all of Egypt.

4 The Journey Completed

Chapter 47 demonstrates how fully God's promises come to pass. Any settlement of people would require Pharaoh's permission. Verses 1–6—Joseph announces that his family has arrived. He selects five brothers to appear before Pharaoh. Pharaoh asks, "What is your occupation?" They reply, "Shepherds … just as our fathers were" (v. 3). This means they will need pasture for their animals. It also provides a reason to request Goshen as a place to settle.

Next Jacob is brought before Pharaoh. Joseph knows the importance of Pharaoh's word. Pharaoh's permission is essential. Verse 8—Pharaoh especially asks about Jacob's age. The elderly were accorded great status in antiquity. Also, in Egypt, a long life meant divine blessing on the person. Jacob is 130 years old. He humbly acknowledges that his years are less than his fathers' (Abraham lived 175 years—Genesis 25:7; Isaac 180—Genesis 35:28). Jacob is aware, however, that he is a pilgrim. He looks forward to a better country than this earth can provide (Hebrews 11:16). Pharaoh gives his permission. Jacob and his family settle in Goshen.

We, with Jacob, are pilgrims. We, with Jacob, look forward to a better country. In Christ, Jacob's seed, we know that it is already ours!

Concluding Activities

As a closing activity have someone read Psalm 133. In introducing this activity, recall for the group how priests of the Old Testament were anointed with olive oil at their ordination. This was, of course, a joyful event for the Israelites. (This anointing pointed ahead to Jesus' anointing by the Holy Spirit as He began His redeeming ministry for us.) Ask the participants to close their eyes and try to visualize what the psalm describes.

After the reading make any necessary announcements and distribute study leaflet 9.

Notes

The Blessing of Jacob: The Line of Promise Continues

Genesis 47:13–50:26

Preparing for the Session

Central Focus

The central focus of this lesson emphasizes God's faithfulness to His covenant promise.

Objectives

That the participant, as a child of God and with the Holy Spirit's help, will be led to

1. appreciate how God provides extra love and care for His children;

2. look forward to a heavenly reunion where all of God's family will be reunited;

3. trust in God's promises, no matter how long it takes for them to be fulfilled;

4. be willing to forsake all and to follow our Lord.

Note for small-group leaders: Lesson notes and other materials you will need begin on page 83.

For the Lecture Leader

This final lesson gives you an opportunity to tie together any loose ends. Place major emphasis on God's faithfulness to His promise, in spite of our unfaithfulness to Him. The Lord is a Lord of grace and mercy, always concerned that His way of salvation comes to pass. It is He who initiates, controls, and guides the affairs of humankind. Trace the history of the covenant promise, showing how our gracious God always managed to continue the lifeline to the Messiah.

Session Plan

Worship

Begin the session with the hymn and prayer printed in the study leaflet. Follow with the devotion. Hymn accompaniments are available in denominational hymnals, such as *Lutheran Worship* (refer to hymnal index).

Devotion

Death may not be the most pleasant of topics. As Woody Allen said, "I'm not afraid of dying; I just don't want to be there when it happens." Nor does having one of the heroes of a book resting in a coffin at the close of that book seem to be an appropriate end after 110 years of faithful service to the Lord. But he has little to do with an appropriate end or even a fulfilling life. After all, a carp can live to be 150 years old, but what human would trade even one second of existence with a bottom-feeding fish? True fulfillment comes with knowing that God's promises have been kept since the beginning of time.

Genesis, by literal definition, is a book of beginnings, but all beginnings must have endings. Do not confuse, however, the Book of Genesis with the Egyptian Book of the Dead. An epilogue of life closes the obituary of each patriarch in Genesis. The lifeline goes on. The covenant promises continue in the messianic line.

Joseph's bones rested in peace in that coffin because he had received the covenant promises of a God who would send another deliverer to Egypt 400 years later. So also, at the close of the Old Testament period, after no prophet spoke in Israel for 400 years, God sent the ultimate deliverer from the bondage of sin and death: the promised Messiah, Jesus Christ.

Patriarchs such as Joseph could rest in peace, knowing the good work God had begun would one day be brought to completion. When our eyelids close in death, we too can rest in God's promises, for we also know the Messiah as our *life* and our *light*.

Lecture Presentation

Introduction

Time. We measure it in many ways. Our quartz watches dissect seconds. Our calendars keep days and months distinct. Our history books divide centuries and ages.

Genesis measures time differently. It measures it by the lifeline. The passage of God's chosen people through time is the story line, the lifeline, that runs from the beginning to the end of Genesis. Adam's generation. Noah's generation. Abram's generation. Isaac's generation. Jacob's generation. Genesis measures time in terms of these categories. The large genealogies serve as bridges between generations (for example, Genesis 5 and 10). Smaller genealogies describe the particular makeup of one generation (for example Genesis 46:8–25).

1 Passages

Genesis 48 begins with a reference to time. It will measure time in terms of the lifeline—God's chosen line. There is about to be a passage from one generation to another. Verse 1—"Some time later Joseph was told, 'Your father is ill.' So he took his two sons Manasseh and Ephraim along with him." These passages are pivotal points in the text of Genesis. The promise of God is being passed from one generation to the next.

So, Joseph takes his sons. He senses that their future place in God's plan will be described by Jacob. The scene is moving. Verse 2—Jacob draws on all his remaining strength to sit up. He repeats God's promise to Joseph. This is the promise God had given to Adam (Genesis 3:15) and repeated in each generation. It is the central thread that unites God's people across generations.

These passages are marked by the repetition of God's gracious promise. Verses 3–4—"Jacob said to Joseph, 'God Almighty appeared to me at Luz in the land of Canaan, and there He blessed me and said to me, "I am going to make you fruitful and will increase your numbers. I will make you a community of peoples, and I will give this land as an everlasting possession to your descendants after you." ' "

The importance of this promise to Jacob is obvious. It provided his understanding of the past. It provides him with a map into the future.

Verses 4–7—God Almighty, who blessed Jacob and his fathers, will also fulfill His promises. Jacob trusts the God who says, "I will make you … I will give [you]" (v. 4). Jacob's confidence in this promise permits him to be specific: Ephraim and Manasseh will also participate in this promise. They will inherit a portion of the Promised Land! Their place in this generation is most appropriate. Rachel had died very early. Ephraim and Manasseh will serve as the sons she was not able to bear.

Verses 8–12—A formal ceremony is now in order. The passage from one generation to another is about to occur. Joseph's sons are announced. They are presented for a blessing. Jacob's frailty reminds the reader that the time is very near. The great patriarch can hardly see. One generation will soon be replaced by another. Ephraim and Manasseh are embraced by Jacob. Then Joseph, with his sons, bows down to receive the blessings.

It is significant that Joseph, the second most powerful person in the world's most powerful nation, bows before a weak and dying father. Joseph acknowledges that God Almighty speaks through Jacob, not through Pharaoh or another power! Joseph's sons are in the hands of God Almighty, not some earthly king!

Verses 13–14—Joseph presents Ephraim and Manasseh so that their blessing might match the order of their birth. The firstborn would normally receive the larger portion. So Manasseh is presented to Jacob's right hand. Jacob, however, reverses his hands. It is God's will that Ephraim should surpass Manasseh in the next generation. God's will does not accord with any human formula. Earlier, Jacob had received the blessing, not Esau. Later, Judah, not Reuben, will receive the greater blessing.

Passages from one generation to another particularly reveal God's hand. His will is made crystal clear in the blessing. Jacob's blessing of Joseph and his sons is such a passage. It is also a beautiful promise. Verses 15–16—"May the God before whom my fathers Abraham and Isaac walked, the God who has been my shepherd all my life to this day, the Angel who has delivered me from all harm—may He bless these boys. May they be called by my name and the names of my fathers Abraham and Isaac, and may they increase greatly upon the earth."

Jacob confesses the God of his fathers to be his "shepherd all my life" (v. 15). Jacob saw God's goodness even before the birth of the Good Shepherd, who would save all of God's children.

This blessing, it should be noted, had legal status in antiquity. The last will and testament of a father to the children could not be changed. This fact becomes obvious. Verses 18–20—Joseph fears that Jacob has made a mistake. Jacob's right hand should be on the older son. "But his father refused and said, 'I know, my son, I know. He too will become a people, and he too will become great. Nevertheless, his younger brother will be greater than he, and his descendants will become a group of nations' " (v. 19). A repetition of the blessing confirms Ephraim's preeminence.

The passage from one generation to another concludes with a touching exchange between Joseph and Jacob. Verses 21–22—Jacob states that he is about to die. But, he also confesses that "God will be with you" (v.21). More than this, God will take Joseph back to the Promised Land. Jacob also gives Joseph a portion of land he had personally taken from the Amorites. God had promised the land. God had promised to be with the chosen people across generations. Jacob confesses these truths in the time of passage. God would continue to be with His people.

This promise came to full fruition in the birth of Jesus of Nazareth. In Christ, God's presence was complete and incontestable. It is Christ who has promised us, "Surely I am with you always, to the very end of the age" (Matthew 28:20). Now, in our passages from one generation to another, we need not fear. We can bless God and bless our children. We go to be "with Christ, which is better by far" (Philippians 1:23).

2   The Great Passage

Bless you! We utter these words with little thought. They are a polite response to a sneeze! We have seen, however, how weighty a blessing was for God's family. Everything hinged on the blessing. Jacob's blessing on Joseph

and his sons in chapter 48 prepares us for the blessing upon all his sons in chapter 49.

Verse 1—Jacob calls his sons together. He makes his purpose perfectly clear: "Gather around so I can tell you what will happen to you in days to come." The shadow of Jacob's words will fall far into the future. His words will come to pass in each of their lives!

Can you imagine the anticipation of this moment? The sons must have been filled with anxious questions. Would their future look bright? Or, would it look bleak? Jacob puts his words in poetic form—another indication of their importance. This poem would be repeated over and over and passed from generation to generation. Later events would bring this poem to mind, for Jacob would tell "what will happen."

Verses 2–27—A poetic portrait of each son is drawn by this blessing. Key traits are singled out. God gives Jacob the foresight to summarize the direction of each son's life in a few words. Reuben, though the firstborn, will not excel. His premature relationship with Bilhah has removed his preeminence. Simeon and Levi, so prone to anger and hatred, will be scattered in Israel. Zebulun will settle by the sea. Issachar will submit to forced labor. Dan will be a model of justice. Gad will live in conflict. Asher will be rich. Naphtali will beget handsome children. Joseph will be blessed abundantly. Benjamin will plunder enemies.

Verses 8–12—The most famous and significant of the blessings is that of Judah. Judah is singled out as the bearer of the lifeline for the next generation. The Messiah will come forth from him! "The scepter will not depart from Judah, nor the ruler's staff from between his feet, until He comes to whom it belongs and the obedience of the nations is His." Judah's line would lead to David. David's line would lead to Christ, to whom "the obedience of the nations" surely belongs.

Later, Moses would bless the tribes who came from these sons. He does so just prior to their entrance into the Holy Land (Deuteronomy 33). Moses blessed them before his death. Jacob's blessing also comes just before his death: Verse 28—"All these are the twelve tribes of Israel, and this is what their father said to them when he blessed them, giving each the blessing appropriate to him."

Verses 29–33—Jacob's death is preceded by a final request. He wants to be buried with his fathers in the cave in the field of Machpelah. The passing of the great patriarch comes quickly: "When Jacob had finished giving instructions to his sons, he drew his feet up into the bed, breathed his last and was gathered to his people" (v. 33). The passage is complete. Jacob is with the God of Abraham and Isaac. A new generation is now bearing the promise. God is with them. The lifeline lives on.

3 An Epilogue

Chapter 50 is an epilogue. Jacob's blessing in chapter 49 has set all things in order. Jacob's death at the end of the blessing concludes the history of the great patriarchs. This epilogue reminds us that Jacob's death is not the end of God's presence with His chosen people.

Verse 1–6—Joseph mourns his father's death. He prepares the body for transportation to the Promised Land. Egypt had sophisticated procedures for embalming the dead. Physicians still marvel at the manner in which Egyptian mummies are preserved. Jacob is mourned 70 days by the Egyptians. Death was seen as a watershed moment. It was not to be covered up and quickly forgotten, as our culture encourages. Joseph then appears before Pharaoh's court, requesting permission to bury his father in Canaan. Pharaoh recognizes Jacob's final wish and grants Joseph permission to go.

Verses 7–13—A large company of Egyptians and relatives goes up with Joseph. The reference to chariots and horsemen suggests a military escort for Joseph's company. Jacob receives an official farewell from the state. The obedience of Jacob's sons is also significant: "So Jacob's sons did as he had commanded them" (v. 12). This is the central emphasis of the closing chapter of Genesis. The last of the patriarchs has his last will and testament fulfilled. Jacob is buried in the cave in the field of Machpelah. This burial reminds the reader that God had promised to give this land to the patriarchs (Genesis 12:1–3). They would all be buried in that land. Their children would receive the entire land.

Verses 15–18—The sons of Jacob now wonder what will happen. They fear that Joseph will avenge himself now that Jacob is buried. They confess their sin and plead for mercy.

Verses 19–21—Joseph's answer is remarkable: " 'Don't be afraid. Am I in the place of God? You intended to harm me, but God intended it for good to accomplish what is now being done, the saving of many lives. So then, don't be afraid. I will provide for you and your children.' And he reassured them and spoke kindly to them."

Joseph sees God's gracious hand even in his brothers' hateful action! The survival of the lifeline was at stake!

God guided Joseph's life so that God's people might live. God's promise of many descendants would come true. Joseph is not simply a model of godliness. He is the instrument by which God saved His people. This people would one day behold that one descendant who would save all nations.

Verses 24–25—Joseph's death is the last event in Genesis. His dying confession, however, points to the future: "I am about to die. But God will surely come to your aid and take you up out of this land to the land He promised on oath to Abraham, Isaac and Jacob" (v. 24). Joseph's dying wish is that his bones be carried up to Canaan when God "come[s] to your aid."

Passages. Genesis has taken us through time. It has measured that time from one generation to another. It ends on the prospect of another passage to the Promised Land when God comes to their aid. The author of Hebrews sees the significance of these passages: "By faith Isaac blessed Jacob and Esau in regard to their future. By faith Jacob, when he was dying, blessed each of Joseph's sons, and worshiped as he leaned on the top of his staff. By faith Joseph, when his end was near, spoke about the exodus of the Israelites from Egypt and gave instructions about his bones" (Hebrews 11:20–22).

God's lifeline is beheld by faith. Faith in God's promise marks the passages of God's people. Faith in the future seed, God's Messiah, would live on in Israel for centuries. It is that same faith by which we now walk. But, by God's grace, we have seen the fruit of the promise. Christ's coming now marks all our passages. As the patriarchs looked forward to His birth, we look forward to His return, when we will recline with Him at Abraham's bosom. This will be the final and greatest passage for all pilgrims who walk by faith in Christ.

Concluding Activities

Conclude this final session of this LifeLight course by speaking a blessing on the participants. Use a blessing from one of the service orders of the church or compose your own blessing.

Announce the start of the next LifeLight course before you dismiss the group.

Notes

Small-Group Leaders Material

The Line of Jacob Is Established

Genesis 25:12–28:22

Preparing for the Session

Central Focus

The influence a godly father can have on his son is awesome. One would assume from Isaac's previous history that his spiritual influence would have been great, but Esau's careless attitude and Jacob's deceitful character demonstrate that Isaac's will was weaker than his eyes. Thus, it would take the heavenly Father a great deal of time to mold Jacob into the spiritually influential patriarch he would become in his later years.

Objectives

That the participant, as a child of God and with the Holy Spirit's help, will be led to

1. observe the influence (for good or bad) that parents have on their children;

2. praise God for continuing the line of promise in ways beyond our expectations;

3. thank God for His continuing protection over our lives, even when we do not deserve it.

Small-Group Discussion Helps

Day 1 • Read Genesis 25:12–34

1. Genesis 25:12–18 mentions the hostility predicted in Genesis 16:12, as well as the 12 sons predicted in Genesis 17:20. Ishmael was blessed with both progeny and power.

2. (a) Both Isaac and Rebekah sought the Lord in prayer. Note how Isaac prayed for his wife. (b) Spouses who can pray for each other, as well as with each other, show a love and concern that binds the marriage together. The husband and wife who pray together tend to stay together.

3. The concept of the firstborn serving the second born was contrary to Near Eastern custom. Also, that the struggle for nationalistic power already had begun in the womb may have seemed problematic.

4. **Challenge question.** Paul points to God's choice of Jacob, rather than firstborn Esau, to demonstrate that God's calling is by grace, not merit. That we are saved is due solely to God's mercy, not our own claims or merit.

5. The name Jacob literally means "he grasps the heel" and can be taken to mean a person who deceives or grabs what he wants from others. The disparaging aspect of his name proved to be predictive of his character in later years.

6. Those who practice favoritism are referred to as lawbreakers. This question may lead to a brief discussion about the inherent dangers of parental favoritism toward children and the effects some favoritism may have had on some members of the LifeLight group as they were growing up.

7. Hebrews 12:16 ranks Esau with the immoral and godless because of his need for instant gratification. Perhaps the "now" generation continues as members of our society seek out immediate and promiscuous sexual gratification, ignoring the risk to emotional and bodily health. The cost of greed may be long-term financial security. Some people discard long-term friendships in favor of brief associations with influential people, who might help them get ahead in the world.

Day 2 • Read Genesis 26:1–35

8. Both incidents occurred in the same geographical area. Both involved threatening Philistine rulers named Abimelech. Both rulers were deceived and took a woman, assuming she was a sister instead of a wife to the respective Hebrew man. Both Abraham and Isaac were blessed with wealth in spite of the deception. However, Abraham had no divine directive to stay at Gerar, as Isaac did. The second Abimelech did not experience infertility, and Rebekah wasn't even Isaac's half sister.

9. Psalm 117:2 speaks of God's faithfulness and love toward us, who constantly break our covenants with Him.

10. God's blessing of flocks created envy and territorial disputes with the surrounding pagan neighbors. Mention that some members of your group may have experienced similar envy, hostility, and harassment from others when God blessed them greatly.

11. (a) Isaac showed his gratitude through obedience and worship. (b) *For personal reflection. Sharing optional.* There are many ways to demonstrate our thankfulness to God for His blessings. Not all methods need be public. The important aspect is to remember to give thanks to a gracious God, no matter how we choose to express our thankfulness.

12. Proverbs 16:7 is an important piece of wisdom to observe among modern believers as well. Isaac's godly behavior apparently won Abimelech over and inspired him to make a treaty that was mutually beneficial. The godly behavior of Christians will win the respect and goodwill of even our unchristian neighbors.

13. Esau's polygamous marriage to pagans was against the principles Abraham had set for Isaac. Isaac wanted his sons to live by these principles too. He knew this would lead Esau away from worship of the true God.

Day 3 • Read Genesis 27:1–40

14. This question is intended to stimulate us humbly to receive God's plan for our lives, since we know that if He had no purpose for us we would not be living.

15. No. God had determined that Jacob would receive the greater and better blessing.

16. Rebekah schemed to deceive her own husband and to cheat her own son Esau. In spite of this cruel trickery God used the end result to fulfill His purpose (Genesis 25:23).

17. Jacob would receive material blessings, political preeminence, and God's protection and favor.

18. Esau's character and subsequent actions indicate regret rather than repentance.

Day 4 • Read Genesis 27:41–28:9

19. The reference is to the anger and jealousy that welled up inside Cain. Yet, Cain's grudge was as much against God as it was against Abel. Furthermore, unlike Jacob, Abel had done nothing to warrant such a grudge on the part of his brother.

20. Rebekah did not want to lose either son—one by murder and the other because he murdered.

21. Rebekah apparently died before Jacob returned home.

22. St. Paul says that they became God's children and they received the divine glory, the covenants, the Torah (Law), temple worship, God's promises, the example of the patriarchs, and best of all, the Messiah, who would come through the lifeline of Israel.

23. We learn that Esau was insecure and thought he could please his father by marrying someone closer to Abraham's line, while still maintaining his other two pagan Hittite wives.

Day 5 • Read Genesis 28:10–22

24. Guilt can only be dealt with by confession and absolution (1 John 1:8–9). If still bothered by guilt after forgiveness has been granted, the believer needs to confront the satanic origins of this false guilt by repetitively claiming God's forgiveness and renouncing this guilt as a lie from hell.

25. The vision shows that God's angels—part of whose function is to minister to our needs—are in constant access to God's throne and are watching over us and protecting us according to His command. Therefore, we need not fear.

26. Christ, who will return soon surrounded by His holy angels, is Himself our bridge into God's presence as He acts as our mediator each day.

27. Jacob received the promise that he and his descendants would one day possess the land, that he would father a vast number of descendants, and that he and his offspring would be a blessing to the whole earth. He also received the promise of God's continual presence

and protection, that God would bring him back to the land he had recently left, and that God would not go back on His word.

28. People who are deeply into the study of God's Word tend to be more prayerful, sensitive, and aware of God's working through daily events. Perhaps we need to ask ourselves at the close of each day how God has worked specifically through the events of the day.

29. Jacob used his stone pillow to make a stone pillar. He consecrated the pillar with oil and named the place Bethel (house of God). He then vowed to give God a tenth of all that he might obtain from his journey.

30. (a) Christians may make vows at Baptism, confirmation, marriage, and on other occasions. (b) Baptismal and confirmation vows are in response to the salvation God has given us in Christ. Marriage vows are in response to God's gift of a spouse.

Jacob's Marriage: The Line Flourishes

Genesis 29:1–31:21

Preparing for the Session

Central Focus

This lesson focuses on a family—a greedy, cunning, and deceptive family out of which God can still bring blessings and a Messiah.

Objectives

That the participant, as a child of God and with the Holy Spirit's help, will be led to

1. learn patience in the face of injustice;

2. praise God for always keeping His promises;

3. grow in integrity, especially when dealing with members of his or her own family;

4. rejoice in the blessings received by others.

Small-Group Discussion Helps

Review question: Isaac knew that a blessing, once given, could not be retracted or annulled. Furthermore, God intended that Jacob receive the blessing of the first-born; Isaac could not alter God's will.

Day 1 • Genesis 29:1–14a

1. Jacob's family raised sheep and other animals for a living. He knew that sheep did not gather at this time of day because the sun was high.

2. Jacob seemed to be helpful, industrious, strong, and emotional.

3. Jacob's arrival must have caused Laban to remember the visit of Abraham's servant, who came with a proposal of marriage for Laban's sister Rebekah—Jacob's mother.

4. (a) Laban must have had hundreds of questions about his sister Rebekah. After seeing Rachel, Jacob may have been eager to share his hope of finding a believing spouse among his relatives. (b) He may not have been as eager to share his role in tricking his brother out of his birthright.

5. Similarities: Here again we have someone from the line of Abraham seeking a believing spouse with the well being where that spouse is found. Both women are beautiful; both ran off to tell parents. Differences: Instead of the servant conducting the search, the suitor, Jacob, does it himself. Instead of the woman drawing the water, Jacob draws it. Instead of a servant bringing many gifts, Jacob brought nothing. Rebekah returned with the servant; Jacob stayed 20 years. Abraham sent gifts for a dowry; Jacob worked for his wives.

Day 2 • Genesis 29:14b–30

6. As a believer, Jacob no doubt was at least partially motivated to see himself as working for the Lord while working for his employer. Whatever we do as Christians can be done to the glory of God.

7. (a) Beauty seems to be the basis for Jacob's choice. No other reasons for his selection are given in the text. (b) God's Word recommends purity, a gentle and quiet spirit, consideration, and faith in Christ as being far superior to outward beauty as qualities to recommend a spouse.

8. Rachel's bridegroom, Jacob, was willing to give up seven years of his life in order to make her his own. But Christ, the heavenly bridegroom, gave up the glory of heaven in the incarnation and gave His very life itself for His bride, the church, as He willingly suffered for her.

9. Jacob, the deceiver, had himself been deceived!

10. Certainly the marriage was fraudulent and could have been considered void. Or Jacob could have accepted the situation and accepted Leah as his wife, giving up

the thought of marrying Rachel. However, at that time (and even for many centuries to come), plural marriages were considered moral and legal, though not encouraged or even expressly permitted by God. Jacob did not sin by marrying both Leah and Rachel (and their maids Bilhah and Zilpah).

Day 3 • Genesis 29:31–30:24

11. (a) God gave Leah four children whom she might love and who would love her. (b) He was to be the son of Israel (Jacob) from whom the Messiah would eventually come.

12. (a) In a society in which children gave women status and barrenness was viewed as a curse from God, Rachel must have felt insecurity, self-pity, fear, and anger at Jacob, in addition to the jealousy of Leah. (b) Several responses might come to mind (continue to pray; submit to God's will; adopt) and may even be appropriate at the right moment. Those who have been in this situation indicate that sincere caring, sympathetic listening, and empathy are most appreciated in this as in other types of grief.

13. When Sarah used Hagar as a surrogate, nothing but grief developed. When we take things into our own hands instead of trusting that the Lord does all things well and that He does them in His own time, we should expect our plans to fall apart.

14. (a) The sisters became bitter toward one another. (b) The irony is that the deal Rachel negotiated so that she might become pregnant resulted in her rival becoming pregnant instead.

15. The irony in Rachel's initial request that God would give her children or she would die is that she died during the childbirth of that second son God added to her.

16. Opinions will vary. Neither seems very spiritual, although it is said of Leah that three out of the first four names of her sons refer to the Lord.

17. **Challenge question.** Leah had Reuben ("see, a son"); Simeon ("one who hears"); Levi ("attached"); Judah ("praise"); Issachar ("reward"); and Zebulun

("honor"). Bilhah had Dan ("he has vindicated" or "judge") and Naphtali ("my struggle"). Zilpah had Gad ("good fortune" or "a troop") and Asher ("happy"). Rachel had Joseph ("adding" or "may he add").

Day 4 • Genesis 30:25–43

18. (a) God had promised to bring Jacob back home safely to the Promised Land. (b) and (c) These questions should only be asked of volunteers.

19. (a) Laban practiced divination (attempting to discern the future or God's will apart from His revealed Word, especially by occult practices). (b) Divination and dabbling with the occult pervade our secular society. Even some Christians cling to their good-luck charms, read their daily horoscopes, and knock on wood as they say their prayers.

20. He was being more than fair, because the majority of the flocks would be solid in color.

21. It seems that Jacob should receive all the spotted animals then in Laban's herds. Perhaps the agreement was that Jacob would receive only the spotted animals born to the purely marked flock. Laban removed all of the multicolored animals, which shows that he was familiar with the laws of heredity.

22. God gave success to Jacob.

Day 5 • Genesis 31:1–21

23. (a) The envy and jealousy of Laban's sons also seemed to infect Laban's attitude toward Jacob. (b) Perhaps this was because, in spite of everything, Laban had seen Jacob come out on top. Laban refused to recognize that God was blessing Jacob.

24. Jacob was concerned about Laban's hostile attitude, as well as his continued deceptions. Furthermore, he now knew that it was God's will for him to leave and go back to the Promised Land. For once, Leah and Rachel were in agreement, because Laban had cheated them also by using their dowries for himself instead of for their benefit.

25. Rachel displays some of the deceptive traits of her husband and her father. She should have had nothing to do with these pagan symbols, even if she were only laying claim to the inheritance.

26. (a) God has preserved the lifeline through Jacob and has blessed Jacob and brought him back to the Promised Land. Furthermore, God has caused the ancestors of His people (except for Benjamin, who was born later, Genesis 35:16–18) to be born. (b) Nothing can frustrate God's purpose to bring about our salvation.

Jacob's Confrontations: Tension on the Line

Genesis 31:22–33:20

Preparing for the Session

Central Focus

This lesson focuses on confrontation within the family of God—confrontation with a father-in-law, with a brother, and even with God Himself.

Objectives

That the participant, as a child of God and with the Holy Spirit's help, will be led to

1. see God's protective presence surrounding us at every moment;

2. experience the benefits of wrestling with God in prayer;

3. learn to confront our problems with God's help rather than to run away from them;

4. celebrate the joy of reconciliation.

Small-Group Discussion Helps

Review question: God blessed Leah with six sons: Reuben, Simeon, Levi, Judah, Issachar, and Zebulun. The Savior of the world would come through the line of Judah, making Leah Jesus' ancestor.

Day 1 • Genesis 31:22–35

1. Jacob's fears proved to be unfounded, for God had warned Laban in a dream not to say "either good or bad" to Jacob—that is, not to entice or force Jacob into returning. Compare Genesis 20:3–17.

2. The departure of Jacob meant the loss of a worker who had brought great wealth to Laban. It also meant the possibility of Laban never seeing his daughters again. But an even greater loss was the loss of face Laban experienced by Jacob's deception. Nevertheless,

Laban seemed to save his greatest concern for last: the theft of his household gods. Evidently, the possession of these objects may have guaranteed Jacob and Laban's daughters a share of inheritance rights from a reluctant and greedy Laban.

3. God has spoken to us through the Gospel concerning His Son, Jesus. This Gospel is the heart and center of God's Word to us. Through the Holy Spirit working in us to understand Scripture, we gain insight into—and are able to evaluate—events in our lives.

Day 2 • Genesis 31:36–55

4. (a) Notice how Jacob's faith becomes evident as he gives God the glory for His bounty and for rebuking Laban. (b) **Challenge question.** A proper fear of God's wrath on the part of Laban and a healthy fear (as in awe and respect) for God's sovereignty by Jacob prevented this situation from developing into armed hostility.

5. Laban foolishly claimed title to property and affections that were no longer his to claim, and yet he wisely proposed a covenant to stave off any possibility of future armed conflict from his estranged family or inheritance claims to Laban's property.

6. Though we may now hear the words of verse 49 used as a benediction or as a statement of love and unity, in their original context they were clearly meant as a denunciation, or curse, that would fall on Jacob if he were to mistreat Laban's daughters.

7. Jesus sealed His covenant, by which He forgives our sins through His substitutionary death on the cross, with the Lord's Supper.

8. Lessons may include learning that God always watches over His people, even when others seem to be taking advantage of them; that our greed can destroy the affections of our loved ones; and that when dealing with worldly people we need to be wise as serpents and innocent as doves. Point out also that God preserved and prospered Jacob for the sake of His plan to produce the Messiah from Jacob's line.

Day 3 • Genesis 32:1–21

9. As Jacob moved toward the land of promise, this angelic encounter was meant to remind him of God's prior promise by Jacob's dream on the way to Haran to always be with Jacob. Jacob did not need to fear. Ultimately, all the good angels are intended to serve us believers (Hebrews 1:14) and to surround us day and night with God's protection (2 Kings 6:15–17).

10. Jacob was no fool. He knew how to cut his losses when necessary. Nevertheless, the previous angelic vision should have bolstered his courage more than it did. Jacob's sinful nature was showing, as it often does with us in the face of uncertain challenges.

11. Verse 9—adoration of God and reminding Him of His promises. Verse 10—confession and acknowledgment of God's previous blessings. Verse 11—petitions. Verse 12—expressing faith in God's promises. The key elements to be emulated and imitated in Jacob's prayer are the humble spirit and the bold trust and claim to God's promises.

12. Probably a case could be made for any one of the three. Perhaps Jacob's strategy could be considered God pleasing if he was trying to reconcile his brother, whom he had wronged. See Matthew 5:23–24. Perhaps Jacob's strategy could be considered prudent in that pacifying his brother would protect his family and possessions. Or perhaps Jacob's strategy could be considered sinister if he was attempting to avoid a just penalty by buying off his brother. Permit participants to voice varying opinions.

13. Taking prudent action (such as posting a guard against an enemy attack—or locking the doors and windows of your home) or working to bring about a desired outcome is neither a substitute for trust in God nor a denial of His providence. We ask God to bless our efforts, then act prudently and work hard. God helps those who in faith implore His blessing on their work. This is what Jacob did (Genesis 28:18–22; 32:9–12).

Day 4 • Genesis 32:22–32

14. (a) The "man" with whom Jacob wrestled was God. (b) We cannot know, but it would appear that Jacob became aware that the "man" was actually God when the "man" disabled Jacob with a touch on the hip. (c) **Challenge question.** This is a difficult question for which the text provides no clear answer. Jacob had struggled all his life—first with Esau, then with Laban, now with Esau once more. God reveals to Jacob in this encounter that Jacob is actually struggling with God Himself, who patiently deals with Jacob in grace and mercy. (d) God lets Jacob know that He could have dealt with Jacob quickly and effortlessly. Jacob realizes that he has been face-to-face with God, who has treated him graciously, not in His holiness, power, or glory. Jacob begs a blessing—and so acknowledges his opponent's superiority.

15. The incarnation of Christ, more so than Jacob's wrestling match, is the greatest evidence that God is always willing to come to His people who wrestle daily with problems they are unable to handle by themselves. Furthermore, this tells us that the reluctance of believers to confront God with their doubts and fears is unfounded. God is willing to come to us wherever we are.

16. (a) Name changes were signs of a change in position or of character. The indication here is that Jacob's humbling admission to being a deceiver was to break his prideful tendency to act without seeking God's blessing first. Now, a new character emerges that seems more willing to seek God's will, even if he must struggle to obey it in order to finally receive God's blessing. (b) Jacob had struggled with Esau and with Laban. Now the struggle would come to an end; Esau would offer no resistance, just as God had checked Laban (31:24–29).

17. (a) God's name is His revelation of Himself to people. God had already revealed Himself to Jacob when He touched Jacob's hip. (b) God has revealed His name to us through Jesus. (c) God generously hears the prayers we offer in Jesus' name (with faith in Him) and responds to these prayers.

Day 5 • Genesis 33:1–20

18. Just as Jacob's parents played favorites, Jacob's willingness to lose Leah and her children before Rachel and her offspring reveals a character flaw that he may have carried to his grave.

19. Perhaps members of your LifeLight study group will come up with descriptive words such as *shocked, dumbfounded, embarrassed, delighted, relieved, overjoyed, surprised, or thankful.*

20. There is no record that Jacob kept his promise to meet Esau in Seir.

21. **Challenge question.** Settling in Shechem instead of going on to Bethel was a serious mistake that would result in tragedy for the entire family.

22. Answers will vary, but our lives are filled with detours that postpone our opportunities to do the things we know God wants us to do now and not later. Fortunately, God did not let any detours get in the way of His master plan to send a Savior into our world.

Jacob's Daughter: Violence on the Line

Genesis 34–36

Preparing for the Session

Central Focus

Jacob's life was a spiritual roller coaster. We sinners/saints can empathize with this great patriarch's spiritual highs and lows. The impact of Jacob's up-and-down spirituality on his family is the focus of this lesson.

Objectives

That the participant, as a child of God and with the Holy Spirit's help, will be led to

1. observe the influence parents have on shaping the morality of their children;

2. rejoice in forgiveness rather than wallow in revenge;

3. Live a life free of the violence of sin;

4. affirm God's covenant grace, no matter what he or she has done.

Small-Group Discussion Helps

Review question: God changed Jacob's name to Israel ("he who struggles with God") after Jacob wrestled with the Lord (who had appeared as a man) all night as Jacob prepared to meet Esau. The strange match assured Jacob that God had graciously caused Jacob to prevail over his opponents.

Day 1 • Genesis 34:1–24

1. (a) Dinah's father and brothers viewed the rape with horror and rage, though their position in that area prevented them from showing their rage openly. (b) Hamor and the Shechemites appear to have taken a casual view of the matter. Sexual promiscuity appears to have been open and not discouraged. (c) Participants

may offer varying assessments. Many in our society also seem to have a casual attitude toward sexual promiscuity and even seem reluctant to condemn rapists.

2. Jacob stopped short of Bethel (Genesis 31:3; 35:1), perhaps fearing Esau (33:16–17). Instead, he settled near a pagan city, exposing his family to its immorality. Dinah, perhaps looking for the companionship of other girls (she had only brothers), "went out to visit the women of the land" (34:1) and so put herself in danger. The guilt of what occurred, however, rested squarely on Shechem.

3. (a) Jacob was one man, surrounded by possible enemies. Perhaps he wanted to consult with his sons or enlist their aid. Also, Dinah's full brothers, in particular, may have shared in exercising authority over her. (b) The challenge to every believer is not to return evil for evil but to practice forgiveness, knowing that vengeance is better left in the hands of a just God. Furthermore, group vengeance usually manifests itself in a lynch-mob mentality.

4. (a) Hamor suggests that the situation be regularized by marriage. He further offered to incorporate Jacob and his family into the Shechemites. (b) The incorporation of Jacob and his family in the Shechemites would mean the end of the Israelites as a separate people through whom God had chosen to bring forth the Savior, who would be a blessing to all peoples.

5. Paul points out that circumcision is valueless unless the Law is kept. Galatians 6:15 affirms that circumcision should be an external sign of a new creation within the heart. Otherwise, it is a painful but useless procedure in trying to get right with God.

6. Marrying in church with no intent to live together with faith in Christ, viewing confirmation as a graduation from all further Christian training and growth, baptizing a baby with no spiritual follow-up are all ways that people commonly abuse Christian rites. Going to church for several weeks in a row after sinning greatly may be another example. The abusive husband may be particularly helpful and apologetic to his wife

for several days after he has beaten her. Someone who has gained money illegally may give part of it to charity. None of these actions, however, will make a wrong action right.

7. The mercenary thought of eventually obtaining the vast wealth of Jacob and of his clan seems to have been the major motive of the people in agreeing to go along with the conditions laid down by Jacob's sons.

Day 2 • Genesis 34:25–31

8. Simeon and Levi—no doubt assisted by their servants and retainers—murdered the men of Shechem. However, the mass looting of people and property by the other sons of Jacob made them part of the crime as well. They became accomplices after the fact.

9. Jacob expresses no regret about the disaster that his sons' vengeful actions had brought on a whole town full of people, only that their rash acts might cause the people around them to retaliate.

10. A thoughtful Christian parent will surely be concerned that a misbehaving child will learn not to repeat misdeeds, that the child apologize or make restitution for the harm that has been done, and that the child show repentance and seek forgiveness from God.

11. (a) Jacob, as he prepared to die, spoke blessings upon his sons. In speaking these blessings, however, Jacob was prophesying under the direction of the Holy Spirit. (b) Jacob's words to Simeon and Levi recalled their heinous act against the Shechemites. As a consequence, their territorial rights were different from those of the other sons in the land of Israel. Levi's descendants were given cities throughout the territories of the other tribes. Simeon's tribe was assigned cities within the territory of Judah.

12. Surely this chapter underlines many lessons we might learn: the need for family heads to exercise godly leadership, the wisdom of avoiding placing ourselves and others into compromising situations, the trouble and heartbreak that vengeance and violence may bring. Participants may also suggest other lessons to be learned from this sordid chapter.

Day 3 • Genesis 35:1–8

13. Jacob's fear of retaliation made him a willing listener to God's voice. At this point Jacob and his clan had bloodied hands (Isaiah 1:15–20) from the slaughter of Shechem and were ripe for spiritual cleansing and renewal.

14. Some objects had come from Rachel's theft of her father's household gods. Other objects, including the earrings (which may have been good-luck charms) may have come from the looting of Shechem.

15. Today's idols come in various forms: addictions, greed, immoral or ungodly relationships, or anything to which one looks as to the highest good in life other than the true God. This false worship can be remedied by confessing our sins to God and receiving His cleansing through the blood of Christ.

16. The external change of clothes indicated an internal change of heart. The passages listed all refer to a spiritual cleansing process—external and internal—that purifies God's people and allows them to stand in the presence of a holy God.

17. Jacob's habitual problem with fear was a waste of precious time. God continually watched over him, as He watched over Joshua and the Israelites as they conquered the Promised Land. God will also watch over us and protect us.

18. As Jesus pointed out, any gathering of His people assures His presence among them. How true it must be, then, for the Christian home built on the foundation of Christ as Lord and Savior!

Day 4 • Genesis 35:9–29

19. Reference again to Jacob's new name, Israel, and to the promises of descendants and land assured Jacob that God had not forgotten His promises. God would honor Jacob and his family as they dedicated themselves to God's purposes for them.

20. Jacob once again set up a stone pillar and poured oil on the pillar to consecrate it. He also poured a drink offering on the pillar, the first such drink offering men-

tioned in the Bible. He reaffirmed the name of the place as Bethel.

21. Because Rachel was Jacob's favorite wife, her death was particularly traumatic for him. Benjamin became an ongoing memory of his love for Rachel.

22. She was buried near Bethlehem.

23. The preeminence Reuben would have enjoyed as the firstborn son was removed. Since Simeon and Levi had also brought themselves into disfavor, the next in line would be Judah (into whose line the Messiah would be born). However, 1 Chronicles 5:1 tells us that the sons of Joseph actually received the rights of the firstborn.

24. (a) Jacob's last stop in Canaan was at Mamre, near Hebron. (b) In a cave at this place both Sarah and Abraham were buried. Isaac and Jacob would also be buried in the same cave.

Day 5 • Genesis 36:1–43

25. Esau acquired a great amount of livestock and became the father of a nation. Kings were descended from him.

26. The land could not sustain the massive flocks owned by each brother.

27. Though Israel and Edom were kindred nations, they were also rivals and were often hostile to each another.

28. Answers will vary.

Joseph's Dreams: Hope on the Line

Genesis 37–38

Preparing for the Session

Central Focus

This lesson begins the final section of the Book of Genesis, explaining how Israel became a nation of people who ended up in Egypt. This particular lesson, however, focuses on the moral tragedies out of which hope for an entire nation would develop.

Objectives

That the participant, as a child of God and with the Holy Spirit's help, will be led to

1. become aware of the consequences of favoritism;

2. view any sin as slavery;

3. understand that the ends do not justify the means;

4. appreciate how God can turn the evil of man to His good purposes.

Small-Group Discussion Helps

Review question: At Bethel Jacob rebuilt and rededicated the stone pillar he had set up there on his way to Haran 20 years earlier. In preparation for the rededication of this commemorative pillar, Jacob and his family reconsecrated themselves to God by getting rid of all idolatrous objects in their possession.

Day 1 • Genesis 37:1–11

1. Certainly some of Jacob's sons had been guilty in the past of violent acts, looting, and adultery. The previous record would indicate that Joseph's "bad report" was no doubt substantive and not exaggerated.

2. (a) Jacob also eventually gave Joseph a parcel of land that he had purchased in the vicinity of Shechem. (b)

Participants will probably suggest many ways in which parental indulgence can hurt rather than help a child. Such behavior might result in a lack of self-discipline, selfishness and self-centeredness, and a similar favoritism in dealing with others.

3. In the first dream, the rest of the sheaves (representing Joseph's 11 brothers) bow down to Joseph's sheaf. In the second dream, the sun and moon (representing Joseph's parents) as well as the 11 stars (Joseph's brothers) bow down to Joseph. These divinely inspired prophecies are subsequently verified by Moses' blessing in Deuteronomy 33:16 and by the relinquishment of Reuben's rights as firstborn to Joseph in 1 Chronicles 5:1–2.

4. While both Jacob and Mary rebuked their sons, they also remembered and continued to reflect on what they said.

5. Joseph told his father about his brothers' sins; he was given a special robe by their father that constantly reminded them of Jacob's favoritism and Joseph's rights of the firstborn (even though he was not the firstborn); and Joseph's dreams may have caused them to feel as if he were lording it over them.

6. (a) The root of bitterness in Hebrews 12:15 and the rotting envy in Proverbs 14:30 are feelings experienced by all of us. Jealousy—the green-eyed monster—arises out of a multitude of emotions, frustrations, and circumstances. (b) Perhaps the most effective method of dealing with temptations of jealousy is to practice becoming a grateful person by beginning every prayer of every day with thanksgiving for what God has given. Most of all, we need to reflect on what God has made us to be in Christ: completely forgiven people, who are now part of God's own people, destined for eternal life with Christ; people whom He is shaping even now to be like His Son (Romans 8:29).

7. Participants might differ. If so, encourage them to give their reasons for their opinions.

Day 2 • Genesis 37:12–24

8. Their previous plundering of Shechem could have made them cocky and bold enough to get into trouble again, or any local inhabitants with long memories could decide to seek vengeance on Jacob's sons.

9. (a) Joseph's brothers plotted to kill him. (b) Most often we tend to feel resentful, hurt, or bitter. Some participants may remind us that Jesus gave His life for us while we were still His enemies, motivating us to be good to those who mistreat us. Some might recall Jesus' will that we go the extra mile for others (Matthew 5:38–48).

10. Neither one was accepted by his own family.

11. (a) Reuben attempted to save Joseph. (b) He persuaded his brothers to put Joseph into a cistern to let him die there rather than killing him outright. Later Reuben planned to come back and pull Joseph out and send him home. (c) Perhaps Reuben, as the oldest brother, felt more responsible for the actions and well-being of the others.

12. God promises to hear our pleas for help even before we voice them; He will respond before we have the request out of our mouths. What compassion the Lord shows to us!

Day 3 • Genesis 37:25–36

13. Modern man also shows a callous lack of sensitivity to the needs of others, looking out for number one, seeing no need to share his blessings with others. As his conscience becomes so seared by darker emotions, he is oblivious to the cries of help around him. No doubt the participants in your group will be able to provide plenty of instances to demonstrate that truth.

14. Among the unrighteous sinners listed in 1 Timothy 1:9–10 are the slave traders. Coupling this with Jesus' statement about sin in John 8:34, we discover that all sinners—including those who trade in human lives—are actually slaves themselves! Sin enslaves people by ruling their lives. The only emancipated people are those made free by the Gospel.

15. Ask your LifeLight group if this question shows a concern for what Reuben will have to say to his father, Jacob, or if this question shows a genuine concern for Joseph's well-being. (The text provides no definite answer.)

16. (a) Answers will vary, but will no doubt include such evaluation as "hardened," "callous," "unloving," and so forth. (b) Isaiah 61:1–3 and 2 Corinthians 1:3–7 show us a God who sympathizes with our griefs and who is always present to comfort us with His love and understanding. Isaiah: God comforts us with the Good News of His love and our eventual release from the darkness of sorrow into the light of eternal joy. 2 Corinthians—He also enables us to comfort and be comforted by the ministrations of our fellow believers.

Day 4 • Genesis 38:1–19

17. Matthew 1:1–3 reveals that the ancestry of the Messiah includes this incestuous union between Judah and Tamar. The sinless Son of God took on our human nature to keep God's Law for us—and to suffer the guilt and punishment also for such gross sins of His ancestors.

18. The three sons were Er, Onan, and Shelah.

19. (a) Deuteronomy 25:5–6 obligated a brother-in-law to provide the widow with a continued family line. Whether due to a lack of concern for his brother's posterity, animosity toward his brother (or sister-in-law), a hope that he would receive part of his brother's inheritance if the widow died without an heir, or some other reason, Onan transgressed the law by purposely forsaking his responsibility. For this, he died. (b) Answers will vary but will no doubt include the "new" sexual ethic of "free" love without benefit of marriage (mutual responsibility) and quiz shows and state lotteries that promote instant wealth rather than responsible money management and savings.

20. (a) Tamar went so far as to dress as a shrine prostitute and locate herself at a place where the grieving Judah would proposition her. She secured Judah's seal, cord, and staff to protect her from the possible consequences of her actions. While Tamar's motive may have

been justifiable, involving herself (and tricking her father-in-law into participating) in an incestuous union cannot be justified. (b) Admittedly Tamar's options were extremely limited. However, she would have been better to submit herself trustfully to God.

Day 5 • Genesis 38:20–30

21. The righteousness referred to in Genesis 38:26 is not the absolute righteousness that is a characteristic of God Himself but, rather, a comparative righteousness, by which one party may be said to act more appropriately than another. In this respect Tamar was more righteous than Judah, because Judah's actions provoked Tamar to do what she did. Nonetheless, neither Judah nor Tamar was righteous in a moral sense.

22. (a) Er's wickedness brought about his early death and prevented him from fulfilling his responsibility as Tamar's husband in providing an heir. (b) Onan refused to fulfill the responsibility of a brother-in-law, as provided by the law of God. (c) Tamar failed to trust God, taking matters into her own hands and sinning against God. (d) Judah refused to keep his promise to Tamar and did not give her his third son, Shelah, as a husband. Also, Judah committed adultery with Tamar, thinking her to be a prostitute. All bore some measure of guilt in this deplorable affair.

23. It is easy to see some parallels between the twin births of Zerah and Perez and of Esau and Jacob. Although the midwife may have considered Zerah the firstborn, it was Perez who was placed first in the genealogical lists of Scripture.

24. (a) The twins were Zerah and Perez. (b) As we read in Ruth 4:18–22 and Luke 3:33, Perez became the ancestor of the Messiah.

Joseph's Temptations: The Line at Pharaoh's Court

Genesis 39–41

Preparing for the Session

Central Focus

This lesson focuses on temptation—in particular, the temptation to seek revenge for past injustices.

Objectives

That the participant, as a child of God and with the Holy Spirit's help, will be led to

1. learn how blessings can come in the midst of trials;

2. see any sin as a sin against God;

3. find ways to serve God under all circumstances;

4. glorify God in times we are tempted to glorify ourselves;

5. let God pursue justice for us in His own time;

6. rely for strength in time of temptation on Jesus, our great High Priest, "who has been tempted in every way, just as we are—yet was without sin" (Hebrews 4:15).

Small-Group Discussion Helps

Review question: Joseph's richly ornamented robe must have reminded his brothers of the favoritism Joseph enjoyed from his father and may also have indicated that Joseph would receive the portion of the first-born as an inheritance. Joseph probably wore the robe constantly, increasing the irritation.

Day 1 • Genesis 39:1–12

1. Success, of course, is relative. The secular world, like the rich fool in Jesus' parable in Luke 12, gauges success by tallying material possessions. Believers see Christ's death as the greatest success story in history and material possessions as rubbish in comparison to knowing

Christ and being assured of their resurrection to eternal life (Philippians 3:7–11).

2. Participants may think of how God has blessed them through their families, their church, satisfying work, opportunities to serve others, or other ways—including, perhaps, material prosperity.

3. Beauty can lead to vanity (Ezekiel 28:17) and to lust (Genesis 39:7), even though external beauty never lasts (Proverbs 31:30). Joseph's good looks made him an attractive temptation for a pagan woman such as Potiphar's wife.

4. Both Joseph (Genesis 39:9) and King David (Psalm 51:4) were aware that all sin is ultimately sin against a holy God.

5. Not only did Joseph refuse her repeated advances, but he attempted to avoid her presence whenever possible. Each of the admonitions from St. Paul's Epistles advocates fleeing from the location where temptation strikes. Many people wonder why they gave in to a temptation when, in fact, if they had avoided the situation from the beginning, they would not have exposed themselves to the temptation or fallen into sin.

6. Do not ask any members of the LifeLight group to share their most persistent temptations, but encourage them to write out the words of 1 Corinthians 10:13 and put those words into their wallet or purse or on their refrigerator. Comfort your group by reading to them the words of Hebrews 2:17–18.

Day 2 • Genesis 39:13–23

7. Potiphar's wife—rebuffed by Joseph at every turn—made up a story about an attempted rape by Joseph. She used his cloak as falsified evidence.

8. By enduring injustice and suffering for doing what is God pleasing, Peter tells us, we will be commended by God for following in Jesus' footsteps of suffering. Also, Jesus says in the Sermon on the Mount that we are blessed and privileged if we suffer insults and persecu-

tion as God's prophets did. We can rejoice in knowing that we will be rewarded in heaven.

9. (a) The Lord was with Joseph. (b) Joseph found favor in the eyes of his master. (c) Each put Joseph in charge. (d) Each master felt no need to concern himself, because Joseph handled everything. (e) The Lord gave Joseph success in everything he did.

Day 3 • Genesis 40:1–23

10. (a) Joseph told his fellow prisoners, who were dejected because they could not understand their dreams, about the all-wise and gracious God. (b) Sensitivity to the needs of others will enable us to show more effectively how God cares about us and how He has met all of our needs.

11. The cupbearer's dream meant that in three days Pharaoh would restore him to his former position of power. The chief baker's dream meant that in three days he would be hanging from a tree.

12. Daniel interpreted dreams for the Babylonian king Nebuchadnezzar.

13. The author of Ecclesiastes views most dreams as meaningless expressions of our troubled, care-filled minds. Both Moses and Jeremiah warn of false prophets, who claim their visions and dreams are from God when they are actually delusions. We now have God's Word, the Bible, through which God communicates with us. Furthermore, dreams were used only in exceptional cases to make His will known.

14. (a) Despite the comfort and encouragement Joseph had given to the chief cupbearer, this Egyptian official soon forgot his promise and forgot about Joseph, leaving him to languish in prison. (b) *For personal reflection. Sharing optional.* Although this question is intended for personal reflection, accept suggestions that might be offered on how to best deal with unkept promises.

15. (a) Psalm 105:18 speaks of Joseph in shackles and irons. (b) St. Paul reminds us that contentment under any circumstance is a state of mind that can be brought about by confidence in God.

Day 4 • Genesis 41:1–40

16. Interpreters of dreams, magicians, astrologers, and enchanters all dealt in the occult as servants of Satan, but these dreams were from the true God. Undoubtedly, God was using these dreams to bring Joseph out of prison and into a position of honor, which would also save the lives of many people.

17. Joseph not only was humble but was quick to give God the glory and to believe wholeheartedly in the power of God to do all things.

18. (a) The dreams forecast seven years of abundance followed by seven years of severe famine. (b) Joseph suggested that royal administrators be appointed to collect a double tithe of all produce during the abundant years to be stored in the cities for distribution during the famine.

19. Pharaoh was so impressed by Joseph's wisdom that he appointed him as chief administrator with authority second only to himself.

Day 5 • Genesis 41:41–57

20. (a) James states God's promise of exaltation to the humble, a truth illustrated by Joseph's rise from prison to palace. (b) Both Joseph and Jesus were subjected to the status of slave (Philippians 2:7), but God elevated them to positions of authority to which all would bow before them (Philippians 2:9–10).

21. Joseph was given an Egyptian name and married an Egyptian. Also, presumably he continued to be clean-shaven—the Egyptian custom. Palestinians normally wore beards.

22. (a) The abundance of surplus grain is described in Genesis 41:49 as being as numerous as the sand of the sea and so bountiful that Joseph could no longer keep records of it. (b) During that time Joseph also was busy instructing the other Egyptian princes and elders.

23. (a) Philippians 3:13 emphasizes the need to forget our past problems (instead of nursing grudges) and to concentrate on our future in heaven. (b) The names Joseph gave to his sons demonstrate that he was grateful

to God, who had made him forget his past troubles and who had made his life fruitful.

24. The people of Canaan, the land in which Joseph's family dwelled, also experienced famine and would eventually have to come to Egypt for help.

Joseph's Brothers: Reunion of the Line

Genesis 42–44

Preparing for the Session

Central Focus

This lesson centers on the spiritual refining process that God used, via Joseph, to set the stage for a long-overdue family reunion.

Objectives

That the participant, as a child of God and with the Holy Spirit's help, will be led to

1. recognize that sin will always find us out;

2. appreciate the processes God uses to change our hearts and bring us to repentance;

3. learn how to love those who have offended us and treated us unjustly;

4. see God's hand in bringing together estranged members of His family.

Small-Group Discussion Helps

Review question: Through Pharaoh's two dreams, God revealed that Egypt would experience seven years of prosperity, followed by seven unproductive years. By enabling Joseph to interpret these dreams, God brought Joseph to become ruler of Egypt so he might provide for his family in Egypt.

Day 1 • Genesis 42:1–12

1. (a) It was a physical famine that brought the prodigal son to his senses. However, Amos says that because drought and a shortage of food were ineffective in bringing the people of his time to repentance, a famine of God's Word would plague the land, and God would be silent even when they called on Him. (b) Both Moses and Jeremiah tell us that God's Word is more important than food and water. While drought and famine may result in physical death, a famine of God's Word would have eternal consequences.

2. Benjamin was Rachel's other son (Joseph's brother), and Jacob did not want to take the chance of losing what he considered to be the last living connection with his favorite wife.

3. More than two decades have passed, and people change. Joseph was not 20 when his brothers sold him into slavery. Furthermore, Joseph spoke and dressed as an Egyptian. Also, none of Joseph's brothers would expect him to be governing Egypt!

4. (a) Joseph was quick to see the fulfillment of his dreams as his brothers bowed before him. (b) Joseph may have thought about how God had directed his life (with its many strange and seemingly wrong turns) according to His will. Joseph voices this conviction in Genesis 50:20.

Day 2 • Genesis 42:13–38

5. Undoubtedly, they must have felt fear, as well as a sense of injustice. They also may have felt homesick and hopeless.

6. At first, he was going to allow only one brother to return in order to get Benjamin to Egypt. However, Joseph subsequently settled for one hostage brother while the other brothers and their families returned home in order to bring Benjamin back to Egypt.

7. Perhaps Joseph was trying to bring his brothers to a point of true repentance, as well as ensuring the likelihood of seeing the rest of his family.

8. (a) Galatians 6:7 reminds us that we can never escape the consequences of our sins. (b) The brothers' spiritual immaturity still manifests itself in their tendency to shift responsibility and not own up to their part in the heinous crime committed against their brother.

9. Joseph wept over his brothers, and he gave them provisions for free by returning all their silver.

10. Such a rash statement could demonstrate a callous disregard for the lives of his own sons, as well as an urgent need to regain his father's respect and trust, which he had lost by sleeping with Jacob's concubine. On the other hand, it could simply demonstrate an overzealous concern for his brother—the same kind of concern he had when attempting to save Joseph from his brothers' hands.

11. Jacob purposely chose to forego saving one son who was not among his favorites rather than risk the possibility of losing a son who was his favorite. Also, he evidenced a lack of trust in God to take care of the situation.

Day 3 • Genesis 43:1–14

12. (a) In verse 2 Jacob tries to ignore the stipulation placed on his sons' return to Egypt. (b) In verse 6 Jacob blames his sons for telling the Egyptian governor about Benjamin, bringing "this trouble." (c) Sometimes people will attempt to deny a problem, hoping it will go away. Sometimes people will blame others for their problems to avoid recognizing or admitting their own fault. Or they may blame someone for their problems so they will have a focus for their anger or frustration. Permit participants to share their opinions.

13. Judah's strongest argument seems to be found in verse 8, where he states that everyone, including Jacob and Benjamin, will die of starvation if Jacob will not let Benjamin go to Egypt with Judah. Judah's personal guarantee for Benjamin's safety, his willingness to take personal responsibility or blame if Benjamin does not return, and the fact that they could have gone to Egypt and have been back twice by this time probably were not as persuasive to Jacob.

14. (a) Jacob no doubt hoped his gifts might turn aside the Egyptian governor's suspicion and possible anger and win his goodwill. Also, attempting to curry favor with rulers by giving them gifts was an expected gesture in ancient times and is an element of protocol still today. (b) Jacob had used the same approach with Esau, his brother, on his return from Haran.

5. (a) Only God can be completely altruistic and unselfish, as He demonstrated when He sent His Son into our world as the greatest gift ever given. However, Christians who have experienced God's own unconditional love can begin to learn to give gifts with no strings attached in response to gifts we have already received from God—especially His grace in Christ. (b) Although the example of sending the Savior overshadows all other examples, personal examples may include the gift of faith and eternal life given at our Baptism, the gift of children, a loving spouse, the church family to which we belong, and a good job.

16. Jacob's declaration expresses a desire that God will help him. But if the Lord does not respond to this request, so be it. Jacob is content to place the matter in God's hands.

Day 4 • Genesis 43:15–34

17. Verse 18 tells us their fear stemmed from not having paid for their previous supplies—even though it was not by their own design.

18. Hosea 5:15 shows that the Law causes sinners to admit their guilt and seek God. Christ has taken away the sins of the penitent and also guilt for those sins. Therefore, God promises in Hebrews 10:17–18 that He will not "remember" such sins: He will never remind us of these sins or hold them against us. We do not need to go on punishing ourselves for those forgiven sins.

19. (a) They respectfully explained their innocence in the previous recovery of their money—and returned it "with interest." (b) God was active in the events. (c) Certainly the Egyptian's references to the true God should have alerted the brothers to the fact that this foreign ruler knew and worshiped their God.

20. Joseph was a person with deep emotions and love for his family.

21. Joseph may have been trying to see whether the brothers' bitterness and jealousy over the favoritism once shown to him held true toward Benjamin. Evidently, the brothers had matured.

Day 5 • Genesis 44:1–34

22. Joseph's actions served a dual purpose: they allowed him to see Benjamin once again and further tested the brothers to see if they would turn on their brother to save their own skins.

23. They experienced a godly sorrow and guilt over their past sin of selling Joseph into slavery, but they were innocent of stealing the cup.

24. Judah was willing to be a substitute for his brother Benjamin. Judah's descendant Jesus Christ made the ultimate sacrifice by laying down His life for us, His brothers (1 John 3:16).

25. Although he had watched Jacob endure grief over the loss of Joseph for more than two decades, Judah now could not bear to see his father endure more sorrow over the loss of another favorite son.

26. The fact that, in verse 13, they all went back to the city and were willing to endure slavery (v. 16), when only Benjamin was held responsible by the Egyptians (v. 10), indicates that they had matured greatly and had improved in character.

Joseph's Justice: God's Guidance of the Line

Genesis 45:1–47:12

Preparing for the Session

Central Focus

This lesson focuses on how God guided circumstances to finally bring about a reunion that healed the wounds left by sin and created a new episode in the history of God's people.

Objectives

That the participant, as a child of God and with the Holy Spirit's help, will be led to

1. value forgiveness;

2. understand that God has a plan for his or her life;

3. learn the importance of caring for the needs of one's family;

4. recognize the need to consult God for guidance before acting.

Small-Group Discussion Helps

Review question: Judah offered to become the governor's slave in place of Benjamin.

Day 1 • Genesis 45:1–15

1. Perhaps Joseph was unwilling to show his emotions before his Egyptian subjects. Or perhaps he was unwilling to make public the problems he had had with members of his family. Or perhaps he simply wanted to keep this moment of reconciliation a very private family matter.

2. Answers will vary, but a combination of all these emotions must have been present.

3. (a) Joseph tells us that what happened to him was intended to preserve a remnant and to save many lives.

(b) Joseph displayed a humble trust in God throughout his life, obeying God and being willing to place himself into God's hands, despite the risks. Scripture does not indicate that Joseph understood God's purpose in his life until God had finished unfolding His plan before Joseph. (c) Psalm 130:5–6 encourages us to trust God and to wait patiently until He chooses to reveal His purposes to us. James 1:5 indicates that we may pray for wisdom. (d) St. Paul implies that by being more sensitive to the workings of God in our lives, we will be better able to understand His good purposes and acknowledge His plan for us, even when things do not seem to be going well.

4. The title *father to Pharaoh* shows how valuable Joseph's advice must have been to Pharaoh. Unfortunately, Joseph had missed out on two decades of fatherly counsel from his own father. Therefore, his offer to move Jacob and all his family and possessions to the land of Goshen before the famine grew even worse showed a true love and concern for him and the rest of the family.

5. Forgiveness needs to be communicated through words and actions—even tears—that indicate the sincerity of the forgiveness.

6. (a) Joseph wept, invited his brothers to come close to him, gave God the glory for bringing him to Egypt, permitted the family to return temporarily to Canaan, granted them some of the choicest land in all of Egypt, and embraced them. (b) Answers will vary, but giving God the glory and allowing the family to return home after embracing them would have been most reassuring.

Day 2 • Genesis 45:16–28

7. Pharaoh demonstrated his pleasure by issuing Joseph's family a royal land grant.

8. There was no need for Joseph's family to bring any of their belongings, because Pharaoh promised to give them the best of everything in Egypt.

9. Being a follower or disciple of Jesus means a willingness to leave anything and everything behind that would potentially deny us eternal life. So material things take on a different perspective. They are seen as merely temporary items for use within the context of our eternal goal.

10. They might quarrel about who was initially to blame in selling Joseph to the slave traders or about Benjamin receiving more gifts than his half-brothers or perhaps about what they were going to tell their father, Jacob, when they got back.

11. When Jacob heard the specific words Joseph told his brothers to speak to Jacob and when Jacob saw the carts filled with Egyptian gifts, he finally believed that Joseph was alive.

Day 3 • Genesis 46:1–27

12. (a) Joseph's offer may have seemed a little too permanent for Jacob, who remembered God's warning to his father, Isaac, not to go down to Egypt but to live instead in the land of promise. (b) Just as Jehoshaphat advised the king of Israel to seek God's counsel before moving ahead, perhaps Jacob also wanted to seek God's guidance before setting foot in a pagan land. Undoubtedly, as with the psalmist, Jacob wanted to give thanks for God's goodness to him.

13. (a) Both Isaac and Jacob received reassurance from God in the midst of their fears. (b) The promise was fulfilled when Joseph returned Jacob's body to Canaan for burial. But the promise may also have looked forward to the time when Jacob's descendants (Israel) would return to the Promised Land under the leadership of Moses. Jacob was told by God that the sojourn of his family was temporary and that, although he would die in Egypt, his descendants would return to the Promised Land.

14. Jacob decided to take what he owned rather than leave it behind for scavengers.

15. (a) Jacob's progeny increased from about 70 people entering Egypt to at least one and a half million leaving Egypt some four centuries later. (b) If Jacob could have gazed into the future, he would have seen a nation of descendants fulfilling God's promise made first to Abraham and confirmed to Jacob.

Day 4 • Genesis 46:28–34

16. Our tears may be tears of contrition, repentance, pain, joy, grief over the loss of a loved one, sadness over a soul gone to hell, excitement, and deep happiness. However, our greatest comfort is knowing that no more tears of sorrow or pain or death will be experienced by believers in heaven (Revelation 21:4).

17. Decade after decade, aged Simeon looked for the day when he might see the Messiah. When he finally did, he knew his future and salvation were peacefully secure. When Jacob discovered that Joseph was alive and would eventually "close Jacob's eyes" in Egypt, he too could depart in peace.

18. (a) Anyone who trusts Jesus for forgiveness, grace, and salvation is "ready to die." (b) Someone might be "ready to die," yet desire to live so as to continue to serve God and others. See Philippians 1:21–26. (c) Those who continue to place their trust in Christ alone and what He did for their eternal salvation can rest comfortably each night, knowing that if they do not wake up on earth the next morning, they will certainly wake up in heaven.

19. God's people were to set a shining example for others to seek after. If they adulterated God's rules by assimilating the pagan culture and religious beliefs of the heathen—which was inevitable if they lived among them and intermarried—they could not become the holy and separate people God wanted them to be.

20. Answers may include setting aside regular times for prayer, Bible study, and worship; using money to support the work of the kingdom of God; not frequenting places in which we would not want to be found if Christ suddenly returned; selecting believers for our closest friends, and so forth.

Day 5 • Genesis 47:1–12

21. Pharaoh wisely used Joseph's administrative abilities and was magnanimous in granting Joseph's family land, possessions, and jobs.

22. Pharaoh had already experienced the wisdom and expertise of Joseph. Perhaps he thought these traits might run in Joseph's family.

23. Here is an opportunity for a people, chosen by God's grace, to honor the true God by avoiding pagan influence and setting an example of obedience for all the pagan Egyptians who would observe them.

24. **Challenge question.** Jacob's blessing on Pharaoh showed that Jacob was greater than Pharaoh.

25. As aliens and strangers on this sinful earth—with heaven as our real home—the author of Hebrews and St. Paul remind us of the momentary nature of our sin-induced problems and point our eyes to a trouble-free eternity with God in our heavenly mansion.

26. Each of us has a God-given responsibility to look after the loved ones whom God has entrusted to our care, knowing that our heavenly Father never fails to look after us, His children.

The Blessing of Jacob: The Line of Promise Continues

Genesis 47:13–50:26

Preparing for the Session

Central Focus

The central focus of this lesson emphasizes God's faithfulness to His covenant promise.

Objectives

That the participant, as a child of God and with the Holy Spirit's help, will be led to

1. appreciate how God provides extra love and care for His children;

2. look forward to a heavenly reunion where all of God's family will be reunited;

3. trust in God's promises, no matter how long it takes for them to be fulfilled;

4. be willing to forsake all and to follow our Lord.

Small-Group Discussion Helps

Review question: Joseph did not take vengeance on his brothers because he realized that God had brought about good—the saving of many people—through what they had done.

Day 1 • Genesis 47:13–31

1. First, Pharaoh received all the money from the people of Egypt until they had no more left with which to purchase grain. Second, he received official ownership of all the livestock in exchange for food. Third (verse 19), he took all the land. Finally, the people indentured themselves as Pharaoh's slaves in exchange for food.

2. Leviticus 25 speaks of safeguards that protected people from being abused if they had to sell themselves into slavery. Furthermore, opportunities were available to Israelites for redemption, including required redemption at the Year of Jubilee.

3. God saw to it that His people prospered in land, in numbers, and in possessions, but the Egyptians sold everything they had, including themselves.

4. (a) Jacob made Joseph swear a solemn oath that he would bury Jacob in his homeland of Canaan, where the earlier patriarchs were buried. (b) Jacob believed God's promise to bring him back from Egypt (Genesis 46:1–4). Furthermore, Jacob knew that Canaan was to be the future possession of Israel.

5. Jacob died with a strong faith, worshiping the Lord and blessing his children.

Day 2 • Genesis 48:1–22

6. Jacob's oldest son—Reuben, the firstborn son of Leah—had slept with Bilhah, Jacob's concubine. Since Reuben was not to be trusted, Jacob gave Joseph—the firstborn son of his favorite wife, Rachel—the right of the firstborn's double portion (which would eventually be divided between Joseph's two sons).

7. Jacob not only felt blessed to be able to see his long lost son, Joseph, but he also lived long enough to see Joseph's children, Manasseh and Ephraim.

8. (a) Jacob calls God shepherd and Angel. (b) Shepherd is a royal metaphor that also describes His continual protection and guidance over His flock today. As Angel, who guarded and delivered Jacob from harm, He continues to guard and deliver us.

9. **Challenge question.** Seth is given preference over Cain, Isaac over Ishmael, Jacob over Esau, Rachel over Leah, and Joseph over Reuben.

10. God would be with him, and God would also bring Joseph back to the land of promise.

Day 3 • Genesis 49:1–28

11. The correct order is Reuben, Simeon, Levi, Judah, Zebulun, Issachar, Dan, Gad, Asher, Naphtali, Ephraim, Manasseh, and Benjamin.

Day 4 • Genesis 49:29–50:14

12. Answers may include a Christian preamble to your will; a tithe left for work in God's kingdom; and a list of Scripture and hymn preferences that emphasize the resurrection.

13. (a) Even Jesus shed tears over the loss of a loved one, as Joseph did and as we do. However, our tears over the death of a fellow believer are not filled with despair, but rather with the confident joy of the resurrection. (b) As Revelation 21:4 points out, such tears of sorrow are reserved only for this earth.

14. Embalming was necessary for Jacob, because he directed that his corpse would be taken back on the long journey for burial in Canaan.

15. The huge entourage—fit for the funeral of a royal Egyptian dignitary—that Pharaoh sent to accompany Jacob's body, the faithfulness of Jacob's family in carrying out his last wishes, and the grief they expressed demonstrate a tremendous amount of love and respect for the patriarch.

16. The family first had to grow in sufficient numbers in an environment separate from not only the Egyptians but also the pagan Canaanites.

Day 5 • Genesis 50:15–26

17. Joseph's brothers assumed that Joseph would change his attitude toward them after Jacob's death and seek vengeance, just as Esau nursed a grudge against Jacob, which he intended to carry out as soon as their father, Isaac, died. That his brothers would even entertain such an idea brought Joseph to tears, for it showed that his brothers did not completely trust his word and were reverting to their old ways.

18. St. Paul encourages us to do good instead of seeking revenge, knowing that God can and does bring good out of evil for His people. Think of the good God brought out of Joseph's bad situation. He used Joseph to save millions of lives and to create an environment where God's chosen people, the Hebrews, could be fruitful and multiply. Think, then, what He can do with the troubles we may presently be working through.

19. No matter at what age God decides to call us home, our time on this earth seems brief and filled with troubles. However, we are precious in God's sight, so our heavenly homecoming is also a precious time over which the angels rejoice with God.

20. For several hundred years the children of Israel knew that Joseph's embalmed body sat in a faith-filled state of readiness for God to carry out His promise of returning it, with His people, to the Promised Land of Canaan. Subsequent generations after Joseph died trusting in that same promise, which eventually was fulfilled.

21. Many will refer to the creation account, but you may be surprised at the variety of responses.

22. Answers will vary, but any reference to the faithfulness of God to His people in continuing the covenant lifeline to the Messiah, in spite of unfaithfulness toward Him, might be an especially appropriate way to end your studies in Genesis.